TRUE LOVE
& SUFFERING

"I wanted to thank you on behalf of every woman for looking out and loving her like you do. I know it is not easy every day. Since what happened to the both of you, I no longer aspire for the type of love you see in the cinema but for the type of love you guys have. Truly, keep being you."

–KEENDER BUENO

"You taught me the gentle spirit and iron discipline. You inspire, teach, and touch with your love and commitment to your beautiful wife."

–SHEVAUN WILLIAMS

"The fires in your souls burn so bright when the two of you are together, and it shows in your eyes. Thank you for sharing such raw emotion and the divine aspects of the light and dark side of love with the world."

–LACEY MARIE

"God damn, this is so powerful. Your writing allows no prisoners or victims and is the message of pure WILL."

–HOPE ZARRO

"Through the example of both of you, you demonstrate the beauty in life."

–NEUROSURGEON FOR KAT & PAVEL

"You two are the best example I have come across that identifies true love: your relentless commitment to her and her outpouring of will, power, and drive to live."

–ETNA MARES

TRUE LOVE & SUFFERING

A CARETAKER'S MEMOIR OF TRAUMA, DESPAIR, AND OTHER BLESSINGS

PAVEL YTHJALL

HOUNDSTOOTH
PRESS

True Love and Suffering
A Caretaker's Memoir of Trauma, Despair, and Other Blessings

ISBN 978-1-5445-2396-5 *Hardcover*
      978-1-5445-2395-8 *Paperback*
      978-1-5445-2394-1 *Ebook*
      978-1-5445-2397-2 *Audiobook*

A TRUE STORY.

SOME NAMES ARE CHANGED.

Kat.

Thanks babe, for everything.

CONTENTS

1 CHAPTER 1
I DREAMT OF AN EASY LIFE

3 CHAPTER 2
YEAR ONE—EMERGENCY ROOM AT LONG BEACH HOSPITAL

7 CHAPTER 3
THE AFTERMATH

9 CHAPTER 4
THE WILL TO LIVE

11 CHAPTER 5
LOVE AND BROKEN BONES

13 CHAPTER 6
GOD, GRACE, AND WILLPOWER

15 CHAPTER 7
ABS AND CHAMPAGNE BEFORE YEAR ONE

17 CHAPTER 8
MY TRUE LOVE

19 CHAPTER 9
I LIKE YOU

21 CHAPTER 10
DATING AFTER HOLLYWOOD HILLS

23 CHAPTER 11
FOR BETTER OR WORSE

25 CHAPTER 12
BACK IN TIME TO POVERTY AND ABUSE

29 CHAPTER 13
JOHN E. GREIF AND THE AIR FORCE

33 CHAPTER 14
EX-BOYFRIEND?

35 CHAPTER 15
WE ARE BACK IN THE EMERGENCY ROOM

37 CHAPTER 16
OUR FIRST ANGEL

41 CHAPTER 17
MY FRIEND EDDIE

43 CHAPTER 18
OUR RAGDOLL ANGEL

45 CHAPTER 19
GUILT

47 CHAPTER 20
WELCOME TO THE WORLD OF HELL

49 CHAPTER 21
KARMA

51 CHAPTER 22
**FAIRYTALE MOMENTS THE YEAR
BEFORE THE ACCIDENT!**

55 CHAPTER 23
THE MONSTER HALO

57 CHAPTER 24
THE MRI

59 CHAPTER 25
KAT FIGHTS TO LIVE

61 CHAPTER 26
THE STRONGMAN CRIES

63 CHAPTER 27
KAT WAKES UP

65 CHAPTER 28
FUCK OFF!

67 CHAPTER 29
FIGHT TO BREATHE

69 CHAPTER 30
DENIAL

71 CHAPTER 31
FINANCIAL HELL

73 CHAPTER 32
I WANTED TO DIE

75 CHAPTER 33
HELL AT NIGHT

77 CHAPTER 34
MY TWO BEST FRIENDS

79 CHAPTER 35
MORE SWEDISH FRIENDS

83 CHAPTER 36
BACK HOME AND DAY DRINKING

87 CHAPTER 37
THE ELEMENTS

89 CHAPTER 38
WILL GOD WIPE HER ASS?

91 CHAPTER 39
EVERYDAY HEROES

93 CHAPTER 40
FUCK YOU!

97 CHAPTER 41
**TAKE CARE OF HER OR I WILL
HUNT YOU DOWN**

99 CHAPTER 42
THE VA

101 CHAPTER 43
UBER AND DEMONS

103 CHAPTER 44
PEOPLE ANGELS

105 CHAPTER 45
WHY GOD, WHY?

107 CHAPTER 46
BLAME GAME

109 CHAPTER 47
NO MOBILITY

111 CHAPTER 48
THE PARASITES

113 CHAPTER 49
THE WORLD GOES BLACK AGAIN

119 CHAPTER 50
MORE DRUGS

121 CHAPTER 51
YOGA

123 CHAPTER 52
MY BETRAYAL

125 CHAPTER 53
MY WISE DAD

127 CHAPTER 54
PAY FOR LIFE QUALITY

129 CHAPTER 55
YEAR ONE HOMECOMING

131 CHAPTER 56
NURSING HOME

133 CHAPTER 57
I MADE A DEAL WITH THE DEVIL

135 CHAPTER 58
**WHAT IF NO ONE KNOWS AND
WHAT IF YOU ARE ALL ALONE?**

137 CHAPTER 59
ALONE

139 CHAPTER 60
ABUSE

141 CHAPTER 61
MOM AND SIS

143 CHAPTER 62
GROWTH

145 CHAPTER 63
FACEBOOK AND DETRA

147 CHAPTER 64
NEW FAMILY TIES AND I AM CHANGING

151 CHAPTER 65
WE ARE HANDICAPPED

153 CHAPTER 66
AN ORIGAMI

155 CHAPTER 67
YEARNING FOR TOUCH

157 CHAPTER 68
NEVER ALONE

159 CHAPTER 69
CHRIS

161 CHAPTER 70
CAN SHE MOVE YET?

163 CHAPTER 71
REMEMBER THE ORIGAMI

165 CHAPTER 72
STUCK FOR LIFE?

167 CHAPTER 73
BULLET OR CANCER

169 CHAPTER 74
NEXTSTEP

171 CHAPTER 75
CAREGIVER DRIVES INTO THE WALL

175 CHAPTER 76
FOR BETTER OR FOR WORSE IN REAL LIFE

179 CHAPTER 77
STRENGTH

181 CHAPTER 78
JAIL OR RANGER

183 CHAPTER 79
THE ABYSS

185 CHAPTER 80
CHAI

187 CHAPTER 81
WE HAVE TO MOVE

189 CHAPTER 82
YEAR ONE RECAP

191 CHAPTER 83
GOD, GRACE, OR WHAT?

193 CHAPTER 84
YEAR TWO, PEANUT SHOWS UP

195 CHAPTER 85
KAT'S BODY DETERIORATES

197 CHAPTER 86
DEATH COMES CALLING

199 CHAPTER 87
HOW LONG WILL I LAST?

201 CHAPTER 88
A BETTER MAN

203 CHAPTER 89
BEGGING FOR MONEY

205 CHAPTER 90
NICOLE IS A BELIEVER AND A DOER

207 CHAPTER 91
I REACHED OUT TO NICOLE BEFORE THE RELEASE OF THE BOOK

209 CHAPTER 92
STOP BEING A LITTLE BITCH, PAVEL

213   CHAPTER 93
      I HAVE PTSD

215   CHAPTER 94
      AIR FORCE "LEAVE NO MAN BEHIND"

217   CHAPTER 95
      TRAUMA SURVIVOR MEETING

219   CHAPTER 96
      YEAR THREE

221   CHAPTER 97
      **IT'S LIKE YOU ALMOST DON'T
      HAVE TO CARE TO SURVIVE**

223   CHAPTER 98
      DREAMS

225   CHAPTER 99
      CAREGIVERS

227   CHAPTER 100
      BEGGING FOR CARE

229   CHAPTER 101
      FORGET PRIDE—THIS IS SURVIVAL

231   CHAPTER 102
      FINANCIAL RELIEF AT LAST

233   CHAPTER 103
      SHAME ON YOU!

235   CHAPTER 104
      FORTUNE LADY AND HEALERS

237 CHAPTER 105
BELIEVERS

239 CHAPTER 106
YEAR FOUR, OUR EVERYDAY IS SO FRAGILE

243 CHAPTER 107
WHO TAKES CARE OF WHOM?

245 CHAPTER 108
ARE YOU A PERVERT?

247 CHAPTER 109
ANGEL DE AMOR

255 CHAPTER 110
TEAM HOYT

257 CHAPTER 111
TANIA

261 CHAPTER 112
IT TOOK ME FOUR YEARS TO LOOK BACK WITHOUT CRYING

263 CHAPTER 113
ROSA

265 CHAPTER 114
THE MEANING OF LIFE

269 CHAPTER 115
I ONLY RESPECT TWO PEOPLE

271 CHAPTER 116
FIGHT YOUR INSTINCTS

273   CHAPTER 117
**A THOUSAND MILES AWAY AND
KAT NEEDS HELP**

275   CHAPTER 118
YEAR FIVE, IT ALL COMES TOGETHER

277   CHAPTER119
THE APOLOGIES

279   CHAPTER 120
MY EX-WIFE

281   CHAPTER 121
COVID-19

283   CHAPTER 122
MARTHA AND HEAVEN

285   CHAPTER 123
EDDIE AND HEAVEN

289   CHAPTER 124
GOOD AND EVIL

291   CHAPTER 125
THE COMEBACK

293   CHAPTER 126
DR. MURPHY

295   CHAPTER 127
ANGST

297   CHAPTER 128
KAT WANTS TO DIE

299 CHAPTER 129
TRUTH AND LOVE

301 CHAPTER 130
BACK TO THE EMERGENCY ROOM

303 CHAPTER 131
HOKA HEY

305 CHAPTER 132
BELIZE

307 CHAPTER 133
THANK YOU

309 CHAPTER 134
**A SELECTION OF FACEBOOK COMMENTS
THAT SAVED ME THE FIRST FIVE YEARS**

321 Resource Sheet

323 Thank You

I DREAMT OF AN EASY LIFE

Wife, white picket fence, and PTA meetings. I dreamt of homemade dinners, evenings in front of the TV, and kids. I dreamt of an easy life and got the hardest life imaginable.

WEDDING DAY IN BELIZE

Kat slaps my butt with roses.

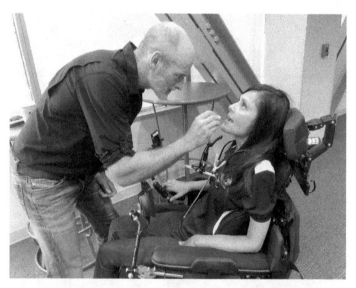

One year after our wedding day in Belize. Kat is paralyzed from her neck down, and I help Kat put her lipstick on. This was right before Kat went on stage to brief about resiliency at the LA Air Force base.

CHAPTER 2

YEAR ONE– EMERGENCY ROOM AT LONG BEACH HOSPITAL

I WAS LAYING ON A HARD, COLD, METAL SURFACE IN THE EMER-gency room, shaking uncontrollably. I was in shock and gasping for water.

I had smashed my head into the windshield and then fallen headfirst out of the Range Rover. In the ER, they hadn't seen that my vertebra was broken, and someone turned my head from side to side while I was lying on the metal gurney. The ER nurse even said, "He seems good to go." That should have been it for me. I should have died.

I was asked to get up. I tried, but I couldn't move my head. Every time I tried to move, it was like an elephant stomping on my head. I told the ER nurses, "I can't move." I raised my voice and said, "I can't get up!" There was silence. Minutes later, I was strapped in with a neck brace and ordered not to move at all. My neck was broken, my skull was cracked, and I was in unbearable pain.

The doctor looked me straight in the eyes and said, "Your wife will be paralyzed for the rest of her life."

At that moment, I didn't know who the doctor was, but when she said it, I believed her. Her dark intense eyes reinforced every word she said.

For some reason, the neurosurgeon, Dr. Nargess, needed to tell me that right then and there, in the midst of all the blood, broken bones, pain, and chaos. This was mere moments after we had gotten out of the ambulance and rolled into the emergency room. Maybe Dr. Nargess knew it would save me. Maybe she saw something in me. Maybe it was just her way of being.

That moment changed my life forever. There was no going back after that.

"Your wife will be paralyzed, neck down, for life," she repeated, and walked away.

I didn't see the doctor again until it was time for the monster halo to be screwed into my skull.

My world fell apart. All my dreams and plans were immediately crushed. There was still hope after the accident out there on the 405 Freeway, but there was no hope after hearing Kat would be paralyzed. Kat didn't understand it yet, but oh, how she would. A flood of tears and screams from the depth of her soul would soon follow.

I had a choice. I could choose to give up and fall into an abyss of self-pity and despair, or I could fight.

For a split second, I weighed my options, and then I started repeating, "I have to be strong for Kat. I have to be strong for Kat. I have to be strong for Kat." I repeated that phrase over and over for three days and three nights. I was on a loop, never stopping.

In time, it got so ingrained in me that I didn't have to repeat it anymore. It was just who I was. **I was strong for Kat.**

I wasn't allowed to move, and I had just been told that my wife would be paralyzed for life. That was three days and three nights I spent in hell.

They had to fuse Kat's spine from C3 to C6 and stabilize the open fractures on her left tibia that had made her lose a lot of blood. Kat was given a 10 percent chance to survive her operation, which took ten hours. I was never told this until years later. I am grateful no one told me.

CHAPTER 3

THE AFTERMATH

There was nothing left of the front part of the Range Rover. To this day, we don't know if it was the car or something on the road that caused the car to lock up and start swerving. AAA took possession of the car in order to pay out the insurance. No one told us to keep the car or have someone look into it. Things were in chaos, and in chaos, only survival matters.

The car after the accident, in a salvage yard.

CHAPTER 4

THE WILL TO LIVE

I BELIEVE WE ALL CARRY THE WILL TO SURVIVE WITHIN. IT'S hard-coded in our genes, but not all of us get to, want to, or dare to open the doors to our own soul. You have to meet yourself naked and be 100 percent honest to harness the power within. You can't bullshit your own genes, but you can harness their power if you awaken yourself and let them heal you by mastering your mind. That is your will to live.

The brain lives in total darkness. The brain gets input from our senses and creates a world for us based on smell, touch, taste, and sight. Our nervous system is a string of thin threads, much like an octopus with a head and its tentacles. So what you tell your brain matters. The brain only knows what you tell it through your senses.

By repeating, "I have to be strong for Kat," I was telling my mind and body to heal so I could help Kat.

It is not the same as praying. When you pray, you wish for something with little to no effort behind it. You are relying on faith and a higher power to grant your wishes and hoping God will act on it on your behalf. When you will yourself, you are actively doing something. You are actively thinking about healing. You are calling upon your soldier genes to go to war against the wounds.

You are imagining yourself healing. You are thinking about how strong you will be.

"I have to be strong for Kat. I have to be strong for Kat. I have to be strong for Kat."

Both Kat and I used this technique, independent from each other, to heal and get stronger. I repeated, "I have to be strong for Kat," and Kat would later practice her breathing in her fight against the ventilator machine doing it for her.

CHAPTER 5

LOVE AND BROKEN BONES

Love got me to fight. Maybe that is what Dr. Nargess saw in me. Maybe she saw Kat's and my **love** for each other.

While Dr. Nargess was a small, intense woman with a serious expression on her face, Dr. Murphy was a big African American man with an infectious smile. He was a bodybuilder type with a real grace in the way he talked and moved. He said he knew there was something special going on, and he went above and beyond for Kat and me.

Dr. Murphy was a Christian man, and I am not, per se, but you will find out throughout this book that I am very spiritual. The way I act in this world is perhaps more religious than most believers, in that I do what I say and not only pray for it.

Dr. Murphy was really a neurosurgery physician assistant, but I always called him "doctor" out of respect, and I still do.

I never understood it when Dr. Murphy told me I could have been worse off than Kat. She was paralyzed and I could move; how could I be worse off? He explained it to me. I had broken my C1 vertebra that is the top vertebra of your cervical spine, the one that controls your breathing and attaches your spine to your skull.

If you break C1 and it is misaligned too much, you don't breathe anymore. You die.

C1 controls your life.

I had smashed my skull into the windshield and broken my C1, cracked my skull, and torn all the ligaments in my neck. Then I had fallen headfirst out of the car after the crash. I got no neck brace in the ambulance, and in the ER, a nurse moved my head from side to side. Dr. Nargess later said, "I didn't know what to do with you. Your head was balancing on a string."

CHAPTER 6

GOD, GRACE, AND WILLPOWER

THE FIRST THREE MONTHS AFTER THE ACCIDENT, I WAS TESTED physically, mentally, and spiritually; right to the edge of my capabilities, and then I was pushed over the edge. I broke down and fell into the abyss, but I came back as a different person. I came back as the person I was supposed to always be.

Call it what you want. God, grace, or willpower. I see this in people going through extreme trauma. They experience a personality change and have a newfound appreciation for life. Even though we are so damaged, we seem to for the first time really see and appreciate life, and many of us are not afraid to die anymore.

To not be afraid to die is the greatest gift on earth. Humans are the only species on earth who are aware of their own mortality, and much of what we do and don't do is a reflection of that. When you stop being afraid of your own mortality, you are set free. I was set free. I was set free to become the man I was born to be. Maybe I had been this man in a previous life, and he was now emerging again. He was in there, in the shadows, ready to be reborn.

I am getting ahead of myself. Let's go back a bit.

CHAPTER 7

ABS AND CHAMPAGNE BEFORE YEAR ONE

LIFE WAS GOOD.

I came to America from Sweden with nothing and slowly built myself up.

I was a fitness photographer, exclusively contracted to work for the biggest fitness magazines in America—*Muscle & Fitness*, *FLEX*, and *Muscle & Fitness HERS*. Besides photography, I helped my ex-wife, Pauline, run a small but rapidly growing fitness company called Fighterdiet.

I was successful at work and climbing the ladder of Hollywood society life. The people at BOA, my favorite restaurant in LA, knew my name. I had a limo driver on speed dial for my dating life, and I had started looking at houses in Hollywood Hills. It was exactly how I envisioned it as I cruised down Sunset Boulevard in my Range Rover, wearing my Rolex watch.

A promo shoot for Fighterdiet, portraying the owners.

I was a perfectionist. Soon I would have to learn to live for the moment, with no perfection at all.

CHAPTER 8

MY TRUE LOVE

KAT HAD CONTACTED ME AND EXPRESSED INTEREST IN HELP-ing out at Fighterdiet events and expos. I remember exchanging emails with her, saying I would be at a fitness party in Hollywood if she wanted to come by and talk. I didn't think much of it until I was at the rooftop party and saw her. My eyes lit up! She was mesmerizing! Dressed in a tight purple outfit that snuggly embraced her curvy body.

Right from the start, it felt completely natural to be with Kat. It was like coming home. We had never met, but in no time, she was sitting on my lap and I was stroking her thick black hair. We never kissed that first night. Kat later said she loved that about me —that I just sat there and caressed her hair, like we had been together forever.

"Do you want to run?" she texted. I said, "Yes," eager to impress. "Meet you at 5:00 a.m. by the Manhattan Beach Pier," she wrote.

I didn't sleep that night, and I was up early, ready to go. Kat was an Air Force major and an avid weekend warrior. She got up every morning before putting on the uniform and going to work to run, swim, and cycle. She had completed numerous marathons, triathlons, and was even a bikini pro in the organization IFBB.

What I was not ready for was a forty-five minute run in the deep sand. Kat left me in the dust, and I was put in place by this fierce and lovable woman. She was testing me; I knew that. I was eager to impress, show initiative, and in all honesty, redeem myself. So I suggested a run up the famous Runyon Canyon in the Hollywood Hills for our next date. Kat accepted the challenge.

The night we met.

CHAPTER 9

I LIKE YOU

WHEN WE REACHED THE TOP OF THE HOLLYWOOD HILLS, WE sat down at a viewpoint, and I asked a nearby woman to take a picture of us. Kat put her hand on my thigh, and I was the happiest man in the world. It's always the small moments that end up being the most important things. That was one. That hand on my thigh was her approval of me. It was her saying, "I like you."

This is the actual moment from that day.

CHAPTER 10

DATING AFTER HOLLYWOOD HILLS

TWO WEEKS INTO DATING, WE BOTH TRAVELED TO LAS VEGAS for a big fitness convention called The Olympia. Fighterdiet had a vendor booth there, and Kat was working at The Olympia too as a sponsored athlete for another company's booth.

I had booked myself into a big room at The Vdara, a posh newly built glass hotel on the strip.

Kat and I lay on the couch together, snuggling, tightly squeezed like snakes. We were silent, looking out through the huge panoramic glass windows at the strip. Kat asked me what I was thinking.

I said, "This is what everyone is looking for, to feel safe in someone's arms."

After that trip we have always told each other, "All is well" in the evening. Reaffirming our love and finding a safe haven from the world in each other's arms.

To this day, I believe that is the foundation of our marriage and why we stuck it out after the accident. We were both looking for someone to feel safe with. Aren't we all?

Kat's comment: "I found comfort in you being loyal and fully dedicated to making me feel loved and secure. We both wanted the same thing."

On that same trip, only two weeks into dating, Kat asked me, "Do you want to go to Belize?" I said yes right away. It was very uncharacteristic of me to jump headfirst into anything, but Kat lured it out of me. She awoke my inner child and made me adventurous. I had to go to my hotel room and Google "Belize," only to find out it was a small country in Central America. I laughed. What had I gotten myself into?

CHAPTER 11

FOR BETTER OR WORSE

KAT AND I LATER GOT MARRIED IN BELIZE ON THE SMALL island on which Kat was born. It was a dream destination wedding with all our friends and family. We said "I do" to each other, and we said "for better or for worse." We just never knew how true the words "for worse" would become, just one year later.

From our first trip to Belize.

CHAPTER 12

BACK IN TIME TO POVERTY AND ABUSE

"La Isla Bonita"—the small beautiful island. That is what Madonna called the island Kat grew up on.

And it sure is beautiful, but La Isla Bonita has its dark secrets too.

Rosa, Kat's mom, fled Honduras, as many still do today, and ended up in Belize at a young age. Living in a wooden shack of no more than one hundred square feet and sleeping on the dirt floor, it was poverty beyond imagination for Rosa, Kat, and Amileth. Amileth was Kat's adopted half-sister and Adam was Kat's brother. Amileth was adopted at a young age and escaped all of the horrors Kat had to endure.

Kat's brother, Adam, outside their house.

Rosa did whatever she could to survive.
Here she is selling tamales from the back of her bicycle.

Kat's childhood was filled with emotional and sexual abuse. She was severely beaten by her mother, and she was also the victim of sexual abuse by her mom's boyfriends. They sexually abused Kat while Rosa worked late nights selling food at the park.

At an early age, Kat was already broken, rejected, and as I can only assume, felt worthless.

Kat told me, "I never wanted to go home. I never knew what punishment was waiting for me there."

The detailed story of Kat's childhood is not for me to tell, but you need to know this part of it to understand where Kat's empathy, compassion, and love comes from. You also need to understand part of Rosa's story, because what happened between Rosa and me is also the story of **true love.**

At only three years old, Rosa was sent to work in the Honduran coffee fields. No school, no childhood, no learning how to read and write. All unimaginable for a westerner. Rosa grew up street smart and had to do whatever she could to eat and get shelter. That was her mindset from three years old and still is to this day. Work supersedes everything for her because work means food and shelter.

Later, Kat got adopted by Americans, only to be sent back home to Belize after one year. The parents' eighteen-year-old son had tried to force himself on Kat, and Kat became rebellious about being there. She got spanked for the rebellion, and she eventually got sent back home. Kat's father, on her birth certificate, was American. His one good contribution is that Kat, due to her US citizenship, was accepted into the US military.

Kat.

CHAPTER 13

JOHN E. GREIF AND THE AIR FORCE

Kat explained to me, "John E. Greif is the American man named on my birth certificate. My mom told me he was my father and she would send me to him when I wanted money to buy chocolate milk and crackers."

John was the one who said, "Here's your plane ticket. In three days, you're going to the US to join the Air Force. They are going to feed you, put clothes on your back, train you, and give you a job. That's all you'll need."

MORE ABUSE

Kat ended up in a destructive relationship in the Air Force, and at one point, she tried to kill herself. She battled her childhood, the abuse, the abandonment, and the demons who lived within her. These are my words, not Kat's, but her words would be worse. She hardly ever talks about it as it brings back too many memories. She tears up and gets quiet when she thinks about it.

At some point, Kat realized that friends are good to have, probably after she found God. I am sure all the trauma she had been through made her want to belong to something and have warmth around her. The more I got to know Kat, the more I saw how consciously and diligently she worked on her friendships. It was and is an absolute priority in her life, and it is what saved us both. Her support system kept us alive until we were well enough to continue living on our own.

I was the opposite. I was withdrawn and antisocial. Kat had to drag me out of the house and teach me how to connect with people. She said, "Ask how they are doing; ask them about their lives; start a conversation." At the time, it seemed disingenuous to me to ask somebody something I didn't want to know. Kat later called me arrogant, and she was right. That was a very hard pill to swallow. It was my upbringing. My childhood home was cold. My sister and I treaded carefully to not disturb the peace. I only have one real lasting memory of my childhood, and it was me as a fourteen- or fifteen-year-old.

That day was no different. Same story, new day. Yelling and screaming and Mom throwing dishes on the floor. My stepdad threatened my mom, and I forget if he did slap her that day or not, but what I do remember is me manning up. I calmly walked into the kitchen, pinned him up against a door and said, "From now on, you go through me." He laughed nervously and ironically, but I saw in his eyes that he accepted it. From that point on, there was a little more peace. He never hit my mom again, at least not when I was around.

Growing up in a very cold home made me long for a big warm family with an abundance of love around me, my white-picket-fence life.

My childhood was in many ways about survival too, but not

in the way Rosa or Kat had to endure. My dad, Terje, instilled a great work ethic in me, and I had very loving summer vacations with him and his mom up until I was sixteen or so.

Now I know it is not disingenuous to care and ask how a new acquaintance, friend, or colleague is doing. To reach out to a new person in your life and try to connect is the most beautiful thing you can do. You are opening yourself up, making yourself vulnerable, starting a conversation. This was just one of many life lessons I was taught by Kat by just being around her and observing her interactions with others.

Kat is special in that way, and she never lost it. Even paralyzed from the neck down, she continues her mission to connect with people and help others. The loss of mobility changed absolutely nothing in regard to her social life. It's all in her heart and soul. All the friends she made from joining the Air Force at age eighteen and on would, twenty years later, help save both her and me when no one else was around. **True love.**

CHAPTER 14

EX-BOYFRIEND?

KAT AND I ARE DATING.

I thought she was going to help an ex-boyfriend, and I wasn't happy about it. I sat next to Kat, loaded with Gatorade bottles in my lap. We were on our way to visit "some guy" who was sick. I asked her, "Why can't he go and get his own fucking Gatorade?" Kat explained that he was sick. I didn't believe it. What the hell? Why did we have to go?

I was suspicious and not really willing to help. It embarrasses me now, but that is how I was. Kat later said that when she first met me, it was "all about me." I am ashamed to admit that she was right. I was kind and never did any harm, but I didn't go out of my way for anyone else. I focused 100 percent on myself.

Turns out the guy was really sick and he was very grateful for us coming, and he was not an old boyfriend. That is Kat. She takes three hours out of her day to help a friend.

CHAPTER 15

WE ARE BACK IN THE EMERGENCY ROOM

They rolled my gurney next to Kat's, and I yelled, "Everything is going to be okay, babe. It's gonna be okay."

Kat responded, "Get away from me," and I braced myself for the storm and the demons to come.

THIS IS HOW THE ACCIDENT HAPPENED

It's Christmastime. Kat had started decorating our Christmas tree, and there was joy in the air.

We were going to a Christmas party in Laguna Beach to visit our friends, Evan and Star.

After picking up Elizabeth, another guest of the Christmas party, I drove onto the on-ramp to the 405 Freeway. Kat was moving around in her seat, looking for her phone to get Christmas music playing. I accelerated, preparing to merge left onto the freeway. Elizabeth says she saw something, but before she could say anything, we all felt it. The car shook violently! It sounded like a huge sledge hammer had been thrust from underneath into our car. BAM!

Right after that awful sound, the Range Rover started swerving sideways, and I grabbed the steering wheel hard. Dust blew up as we drifted onto the side of the road, and I couldn't see anything. I was trying to gain control of the car to get us back onto the main road.

It never entered my mind that we would not be okay, even as we were completely covered in dust, aimlessly drifting at high speed. Later, Kat said the same thing: she wasn't afraid. Why we weren't afraid, I don't know. We should have been.

Without warning, my head was thrust sideways into the windshield, and I broke my neck. Before I blacked out, I remember thinking, "This is going to hurt." I think I had a sense that we would crash, but I could have never imagined the tragic outcome. I still believed it would just hurt badly but not be life altering.

The car had rammed into a street sign on the side of the road, and the Range Rover had started to roll uncontrollably. My world was black. I was unconscious after breaking my neck.

Elizabeth, our passenger, says we rolled three to four times until we landed upside down, pinned down by the safety railing on the side of the road. The car was balancing upside down in midair over a grassy hill. The Range Rover's headlights were illuminating the treetops.

I was later billed by the city of Long Beach for hitting the street sign. The world showed no mercy.

CHAPTER 16

OUR FIRST ANGEL

I REGAINED CONSCIOUSNESS AS WE WERE HANGING UPSIDE down. The seat belt had saved me from falling out while unconscious and decapitating myself.

I looked over at Kat and screamed at her, "Are you okay, are you okay?" She immediately responded, "Get help, I have broken my arms!" She had not broken her arms; she had broken her neck instantly on impact. The Range Rover had landed on Kat's side, and she never had a chance. Kat's side took all of the impact and crushed her side of the car.

Kat didn't know it, but her tibia was broken too, white bone penetrating her skin, pulsating blood and draining her of her life. Her tibia was crushed in several places from hitting the dashboard each time the Range Rover rolled over. She later said she felt life slipping away and that she was ready to die, like so many times before in her life.

I unbuckled my seat belt and fell straight down, out of the shattered car window onto a grassy hill. I was dazed and there was blood and glass everywhere.

In war movies, after a bomb goes off, they often show the soldier from his point of view with a wide angle lens, making everything around the soldier distorted and blurry. That is exactly how it felt.

You are looking around to find your bearings. You are looking for a foothold, while your vision and hearing are going haywire. It's like having vertigo on a ship in the high seas.

Kat again said in a calm but firm, loud voice, "Call for help."

I looked through my pockets—no phone.

I yelled, "I can't find my phone."

Kat was in the car with Elizabeth looking for their phones and a way to get out of the car. Kat couldn't get her hands on the seat belt. Something was wrong, but she didn't know what. She told Elizabeth her arms were broken and that she couldn't unstrap herself from the seat belt.

Elizabeth handed me her purse through the back seat car window as she couldn't get out of the car. I poured the contents on the ground, but my brain couldn't comprehend what a phone looked like.

"I can't find it," I screamed to Kat. "I can't find it."

I panicked. I literally could not remember what a phone looked like. My brain was not right.

"Go and get help," Kat said, this time chillingly clear. Her Air Force training was on full display. I walked on the side of the highway, frantically waving my hands. Six highway lanes filled with cars flying by me, and no one stopped or slowed down. Just lights and the sound of cars flying by—swish, swish, swish.

I felt my life slipping away. All I wanted to do was lie down on the grass and sleep, but I knew what that meant. Death.

I couldn't make out any faces, just lights. That was when I decided I was ready to die for Kat. It was the moment I knew what **true love** was. I walked out onto the 405 Freeway, against the oncoming lanes of traffic, ready to be hit and die. Three lanes of fast-moving cars were coming right at me. They honked their horns, swerved around me, but no one stopped.

I felt myself fading fast. I needed to get help.

You may ask, how did I know I was about to die? Trust me, you know. You know when your time is running out.

CHAPTER 17

MY FRIEND EDDIE

EDDIE KNEW HIS TIME WAS UP TOO AND ASKED THE NURSES to stop all life-sustaining treatment. I stood next to his hospital bed and watched him die while Kat cried. Speaking softly, she said, "I'm sorry, Eddie. I'm sorry."

We had met Eddie the night of our accident. Before we drove out, we had attended a small, private party in Manhattan Beach, and I met Eddie there for the first time. We immediately connected, and I said I wished we could stay. I would have much rather hung out with him and his friends. Most were active duty Air Force and Air Force veterans, all having a good time.

Three years after we met at that small party, we were saying our goodbyes to Eddie, lives intertwined in such a way you start to wonder about God, demons, and everything in between. It gives me great comfort that Eddie was a religious man and that he found comfort in the Bible. He died in peace with the love of his life, Neva, next to him.

I will get back to Eddie later in my story, but everything Kat's friends did to keep me alive and healthy, I tried to pay forward to Eddie. I needed to prove to myself that I could help others as I would have wanted my best friends and family to help me.

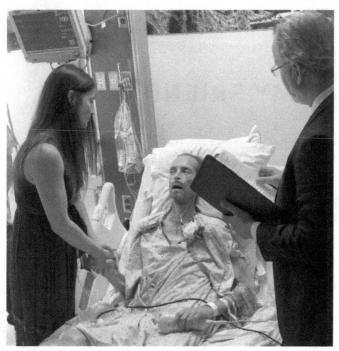

Eddie and Neva got married in the ICU.
Eddie passed away the day after their marriage.

CHAPTER 18

OUR RAGDOLL ANGEL

WE ARE BACK AT THE ACCIDENT SCENE

I WAS WALKING ON THE SIDE OF THE ROAD, SCREAMING OUT for help!

Dressed like a ragdoll covered in blankets, he appeared out of nowhere. "Do you need help?" he asked.

"Yes, call 911!"

He nodded and disappeared. Our angel was a homeless man living beneath the highway pass. Years later, Kat drove by, and she said he was still there. I haven't gone back to the accident scene yet. I can't, but I know I will one day before this book is published.

My head was pounding badly. I remember thinking, "Kat is going to be so pissed about her broken arms," and God, how I wish it would have been just broken arms. That would have been a blessing.

I heard the sirens in the distance, and soon after, I was lying in an ambulance, screaming at the police officer and EMT inside because I couldn't hear myself talk.

Kat is my hero. Her Air Force training kept her calm, and it guided me to look for help. It kept me alive and focused.

Kat saved us.

CHAPTER 19

GUILT

THE FIRST QUESTION THE POLICE OFFICER ASKED ME WAS, "Were you drinking?" Then the EMT asked, "Alcohol?" and then the Air Force investigators wanted to know, and then the whole world wanted to know. No, I was not drinking. Not a single drop, and the blood test proved it.

Almost immediately after the blood test came back, everyone wrote it off as an accident, which it was, but the guilt and condemnation were still there.

My guilt toward myself and other people's guilt toward me. They were blaming me because they had to guilt someone. They couldn't just write it off as an accident. Someone had to take the blame, and things were about to turn really ugly.

CHAPTER 20

WELCOME TO THE WORLD OF HELL

As soon as the morphine hit my bloodstream, I puked all over myself. My body couldn't handle it, and it went on like that for days. I didn't have any friends at the hospital, but Kat's Air Force colleagues held my head up when it was time to puke. One of them was Ivan. He never budged. Military men are trained for this.

I was not allowed to move. Any movement could paralyze me or more likely kill me, but I couldn't help convulsing heavily as my guts came flying out when the morphine was pushed into my bloodstream.

Kat was out of surgery, in a coma-like state. A ventilator machine was breathing for her and tubes were feeding her. No one knew if she would ever breathe on her own, let alone move again. And if she woke up, no one knew if she'd still be Kat, if her soul and brain were intact, or if she was just a "vegetable."

Kat primarily damaged her nerves at the fourth and fifth cervical vertebrae. The neurosurgeon inserted hardware to fuse her spine from C3 down to C6. She then went under an orthopedic surgery to have a metal rod with seven screws placed in her left tibia to hold her leg in place. The nurses, coordinators, and doctors all saw something in us and went above and beyond the call of duty to save us. I'd like to think they saw **love and hope**, and they wanted to save it. It's so precious, rare, and fragile.

CHAPTER 21

KARMA

THE TIME BETWEEN KAT'S SURGERY AND WHEN SHE FINALLY opened her eyes was my worst. Did I cause this?

I replayed the accident a million times in my head. When I was sleeping, my brain went all the way back to my childhood, and year for year, it went over all significant and random events in my life. I know this because I remember it. My brain was looking for a reason from my past as to why this had happened. My brain was trying to save me from falling into the abyss. Was this accident my karma?

I scorched myself thinking about the accident over and over. I was so angry at the world! After one week, I accepted the fact that the world is filled with randomness, and it was an accident. That made me move on. That made me at least take a step back from the ledge of the abyss.

Elizabeth, our passenger, had been taken to another hospital. She was okay. The back of the car was relatively unharmed, and she got away with a few scratches. I only saw Elizabeth once after the accident. I don't blame her for not being a part of our lives. We would just be a constant reminder of a terrible night to her.

CHAPTER 22

FAIRYTALE MOMENTS THE YEAR BEFORE THE ACCIDENT!

It was a fairytale. Don't get me wrong; there were fights, really intense ones, but we always showed our love and respect for one another. We competed in loving each other more (and still do). We always tried to outdo ourselves in gifts and surprises!

My best friend Ted said, "She is good for you," and yes, she was. Kat took a shy Swedish boy and made him appreciate life. I would have died unfulfilled without her. I recognized that early on, and that is the biggest reason I am still here today. I owe Kat so much for making me see life, for helping me become the best version of myself. And by becoming the best version of myself, I help others. It was in me; I just never knew how to bring it out of me.

When Kat deployed to Kyrgyzstan, I had a propeller plane write, "Papi loves Kat" in white smoke against a dark blue sky seen all over Los Angeles. Kat surprised me by bringing my dad over from Norway (he hates traveling). I rented a helicopter that landed in the Santa Monica mountains for a picnic with champagne and strawberries. I chartered Los Angeles's biggest yacht, where I proposed to Kat in front of twelve of our closest friends, all dressed in white. We went to explore Belize after only knowing each other for two weeks.

It was wild, crazy, and fun. Kat made me feel adventurous.

I had a plane write "Papi loves Kat" all over the sky when Kat was deployed to Kyrgyzstan.

Sharing a hammock in Belize.

The day I asked Kat to marry me. First, champagne brunch on a mountain top, and then I rented Los Angeles's biggest charter yacht, where I asked for her hand while cruising outside LA in a white yacht and all guests dressed in white.

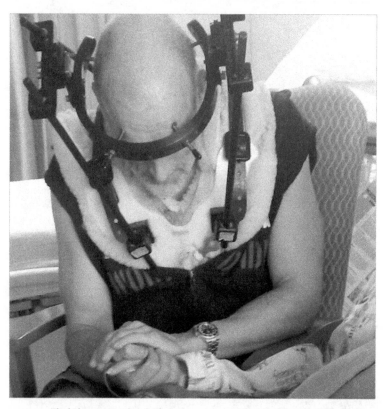

The halo is put in place by four screws, screwed directly into your skull.
The monster halo is worn twenty-four/seven for months.

CHAPTER 23

THE MONSTER HALO

It was day three at the Long Beach Intensive Care Unit.

Dr. Nargess later said she had never seen anything like it. My head was balancing on a string and literally separating from my body. I should have been dead. Even to this day, I don't know why I survived.

The luck of the draw?

Dr. Nargess didn't know what to do with me. I was ordered to lie absolutely still in the hospital bed, and I mean absolutely still. For three days, I laid like that. Frozen in time, thinking about Kat, awaiting my destiny.

Finally, the doctor decided to take a chance with me and screwed a monster halo into my skull, giving me a chance at a normal life instead of an operation. An operation could mean paralysis, restricted movement, or death. The doctor knew someone had to take care of Kat, so I think she wanted to give me a chance.

Four people were in the room, and many more were outside looking in because the halo, the metal monster, doesn't happen every day. I only knew I was going to get something, but I had no concept of what the halo was. I was soon to find out what torture is.

Dr. Nargess naturally demands respect wherever she goes. She has a way about her, and her small stature is in no way a hindrance for her. She commands her troops and they obey! Dr. Nargess walked straight up to me, took my hands in hers and said, "Be brave," and she never let go of me with her eyes. The halo is normally placed when someone is under anesthesia, but I was wide awake.

The screws are regular Home Depot screws drilled into your skull with a regular Home Depot screwdriver. Four of them! While trying not to pass out, I had to stretch out my arms and make fists with my hands so the doctor could see that no nerves got damaged while she physically and literally pressed my head down onto my spine. They tightened the screws, shot me full of pain meds, and I collapsed into a wheelchair.

I woke up and had to fight off a panic attack! My head was fixed so I could only look straight ahead. To turn, I had to turn my whole body. I could not look down or up, just straight ahead. The urge to get out of the monster halo was overwhelming, and I had to calm myself down by talking to myself and taking deep breaths.

CHAPTER 24

THE MRI

NEXT STOP. THE MRI.

The Long Beach hospital is a huge place with a labyrinth of corridors and small rooms. I was dazed and tired from the halo. I was lying on a metal gurney, alone. My gurney was shoved off to the side, against a gray faded wall. I was still repeating, "I have to be strong for Kat." Having a purpose helped me not to focus on my own mental and physical pain.

The technician came out, wheeled me into the MRI room, and explained what was going to happen. This was probably his thousandth time, but this time was to be different for him and a nightmare come true for me. It was meant to be routine. Wheel me in, check that the halo was fixing my vertebrae correctly so they could fuse back together, and then wheel me out.

Inside the full body MRI, I laid completely still. I was tired and I relaxed my whole body.

The machine started. It makes an awful sound, almost alien-like. That didn't bother me, but I felt my head getting warmer. I told myself I was imagining it and tried to relax. Inside my head, the warm sensation slowly became a burning sensation, and that is when I panicked and started screaming.

"HELP!"

A monotone voice came on over the loudspeaker, "How are you doing?"

I replied, "I am burning. Get me out of here!"

There was a moment of disbelief on the other end, because nothing happened, just silence. I screamed louder and now I was afraid for my life.

"HELP!"

My brain was heating up. I was being cooked from the inside out!

"HELLLLP!"

Finally, the machine stopped humming, and the technician wheeled me out.

I felt the outside of the screws with my hand and the technician felt them too. We looked at each other. The screws were hot! He quickly ran off to make a phone call. This was never mentioned in any of my hospital reports. The screws that secured the halo into my skull had heated up and burned me from the inside of my skull.

I never took this any further. With my broken neck, a monster halo on my head, and my wife paralyzed, I had enough to think about. I later found out that the metal alloy of the screws was not meant for an MRI machine. A friend of mine working for a big medical device company told me.

CHAPTER 25

KAT FIGHTS
TO LIVE

KAT SURVIVED THE INITIAL TEN-HOUR SURGERY AND WAS IN a coma-like state in the ICU.

Laura, our hospital coordinator, broke the hospital rules about visiting in the ICU. She put me in a wheelchair and wheeled me up to the ICU where Kat was. I knew why. Kat was in that place between life and death, and maybe me being by her side could sway her to choose life. This was the first time I saw her after she told me to stay away in the emergency room.

Kat looked so fragile, tubes and machines everywhere. I was immediately overwhelmed with love for her. I hated myself and the world for this happening to us. I sat in my wheelchair, crying. I managed to slowly rise up out of my wheelchair and yelled, "Fight for us, Kat! You fight for us!" I was very loud, but the nurses let me scream. They understood. I yelled again and again. I was in severe pain and my legs wouldn't carry me very long. I sat back down.

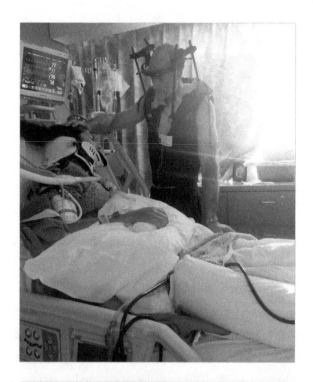

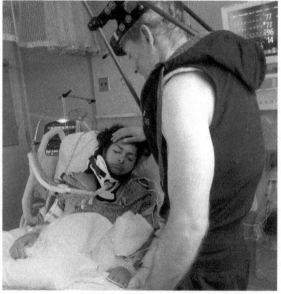

CHAPTER 26

THE STRONGMAN CRIES

I LOOKED UP AT COLONEL WASSON, AND TEARS ROLLED DOWN this strong, proud, military man's face.

Colonel Wasson had been Kat's mentor and coached her how to run fast marathons and to always finish strong. He had flown in from Colorado where he was stationed, and now he was asking Kat for one final race, to finish strong. He said it out loud, "One more race, Kat, just one more."

And maybe she heard him.

Kat did wake up. Not then, but shortly thereafter.

It was day three in the ICU, and it took me three years from that day to start writing this book. It took three years to get to our "new normal." It took three years to dare to look up, look ahead, and make plans for the future.

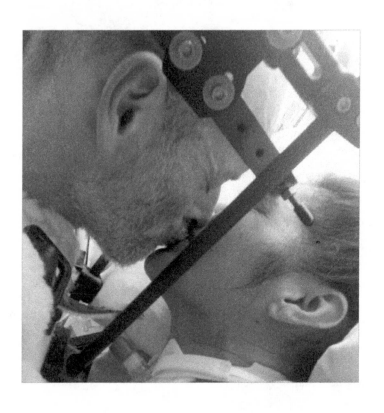

CHAPTER 27

KAT WAKES UP

When Kat woke up, her mind saved her from realizing what had happened to her. It took months for her mind to slowly accept her new reality. Her unconscious self saved her conscious self from taking it all in at once. It would have been too much to bear. I was nervous to see her. The last time she saw me in the emergency room, she had told me to "get away," but Kat was happy to see me. We cried together.

Comment from Kat: "I remember waking up and thinking about my husband. Where was he? When Pavel came walking in, I had a huge smile on my face."

CHAPTER 28

FUCK OFF!

I said, "Stop taking pictures," and delete the ones on Facebook!

Kat had just woken up from her coma and was fighting to hold onto her life. Everyone wanted a selfie with Kat, and she was always eager to please. She smiled but got exhausted fast.

I told more people to "fuck off" than I can remember that first week in the hospital. I was angry at the world and asking myself why. How could this be real? I tried to turn back time, with will, with prayers, with screams from the depth of my core, but the world kept spinning around the sun as it always has.

My ego refused to accept this new reality. My ego already had my whole life planned out for me, and this was not it. I was raging against the world, against God, against everything. I had worked so hard to achieve everything I had. I had the perfect life. I was angry at everyone—hospital staff, friends, and visitors. It lasted months, and if I am really honest, years.

A couple of days after the halo was drilled into my skull, I was able to stand on my feet. I was encouraged to start taking small steps around the room, down the corridor, and finally around the hospital.

It's a strange feeling when you know you are going to live but you are half dead. I could feel that I was going to be fine. I didn't know it then, but the journey to full recovery would take years. I did recuperate and became physically stronger than ever, but then and there in the hospital hallways, it wasn't my body I was fighting. It was my demons, and I am still fighting them. I think I always will be.

They say time heals all wounds, but that is not actually true. What happens is that you learn to live with it. The ones who don't learn to live with it, more than often, take their own lives. You see, what kills people is the pain. They can't endure the heartache anymore. I know; I was there, looking down into the abyss.

I was bombarded with hospital forms from the hospital administrator. I was Kat's husband, and I had to approve every procedure. Her tibia needed repair, hyperbaric chamber, insurance papers—oh God, were there insurance papers. Even to this day, five years after, sporadic bills keep coming. I have stopped paying them. The debt collectors eventually stopped calling too.

CHAPTER 29

FIGHT TO BREATHE

KAT WAS STILL KAT. A VENTILATOR WAS BREATHING FOR HER, but the physical hole and the inserted plastic valve in her throat prevented her from speaking. She got so mad at me when I didn't understand what she wanted. There was a fire in her eyes when I couldn't read her lips correctly. Kat's expressive face to this day is a blessing. She now points with her lip and uses her facial expressions to elaborate a comment since she can't use her hands.

She asked for tea and fruit when asked if she needed anything. She had not processed that she was surviving via a machine and was getting liquid nutrients via a feeding tube.

Kat would have been on a breathing tube to this day if it weren't for one person: respiratory physician Tom. He saw the support from Kat's Air Force wingmen and overheard that Kat was a triathlete. He saw in Kat what I saw and others knew Kat to be—a warrior. Tom fought the other doctor's orders, and he and Kat secretly worked at improving Kat's breathing. Tom figured out that a different valve could be put in place at certain hours of the day to allow Kat to speak.

This all occurred pre-pandemic, when resources were plenty in the hospital and Kat was covered by Tricare, her military insurance, which guarantees payment. But even then, we had to fight for Kat's right to breathe on her own. It turns out, I wasn't alone. Detra, a saving angel, would later tell me the same story about how she had to fight the doctors to save her daughter, Jo-Jo. Good people fought for us—that is why we are here today. And we fought for ourselves—that is also why we are here today.

The training started with Kat lying awake all night thinking about breathing. Just like I had thought, "I have to be strong for Kat," Kat was now actively thinking "Breathe in, breathe out, breathe in, breathe out." She did three sets of fifteen repetitions, just like when she weight trained at the gym. Tom slowly weaned Kat of the amount of oxygen the machine was providing for her, and slowly Kat replaced the machine oxygen with her own breathing. This was no small feat! Kat's warrior spirit and the physician believing in her made it happen. Eventually the other doctors could not say no. Kat was given the permission to take out the plastic valve, and she could start breathing on her own.

I want to emphasize Kat's will to live. Her will is very strong, as you will find out throughout this book. A lesser person would never have gotten off the ventilator. Today, Kat's lungs are at about 40 percent capacity. She can only speak a few sentences at a time, and she takes deep breaths to assist her voice, which is very weak.

CHAPTER 30

DENIAL

A FEW WEEKS AFTER THE ACCIDENT, I SAT AT THE EDGE OF the hospital bed.

Kat looked at me, smiled, took a breath in, and said, "We may have to wait to move to Vandenberg."

Kat was supposed to be transferred from Los Angeles Air Force Base to Vandenberg Air Force Base that year. I looked at Kat, nodded, and smiled.

I said, "Yes, babe, no problem."

We were in her hospital room, and Kat was in full denial. Her mind would not let her understand that she was paralyzed yet. She told her coworkers that she would be out of office for about six months but that she would be back to work.

CHAPTER 31

FINANCIAL HELL

I WAS WANDERING THE HOSPITAL HALLWAYS WHEN DR. Murphy called my name, "Pavel." He held out an envelope and said, "I talked to my wife last night, and we agreed you should have this. I have been saving for my dream watch, but you know you will need this."

At that moment, I didn't know what he was referring to, but I took the envelope out of respect for Dr. Murphy. He gave me $1,000 in cash. His hard-earned savings for a dream watch. I didn't know why I would need it, but it would soon become very clear.

Estimated costs for someone with paralysis like Kat is about $1.1 million the first year and $200,000 the subsequent years for 24/7 care, until death. Lifetime costs are around $3–4 million depending on individual circumstances. I didn't know this. I had no idea of the financial hell I was in for.

Does life have a price? Oh yes, it does. When your pet gets sick, how much are you willing to spend? $100. $500. $1,000. $4,000? How much? When is it too much? Trust me, you will reach a number when it is too much, and that is the cost of a life.

I took the envelope, and just a few months later, Dr. Murphy got his watch in an unexpected way. God, grace, karma, pay it forward, call it what you will.

CHAPTER 32

I WANTED TO DIE

I WANTED TO DIE FROM THE HEARTACHE OF SEEING KAT'S whole world slowly go under. Or more correctly, I wanted to die to not have to experience Kat's pain; that is more truthful. All that she had worked so hard for was taken from her. Her career, her athletic achievements, her dreams.

Dr. Murphy was the one who told her. He was gentle but honest.

"I will never be able to move?" Kat asked.

"Based on the cases I have seen, and the severity of your injury, there is a very slim chance," Dr. Murphy said.

I just sat there, in my halo, trying to absorb as much pain as possible, but this pain was all Kat's. This was her judgment day. She put on a brave face that day. The analytical and intellectual Kat came out. The screams and death wishes would come later, at night in the hospital bed at the VA and when she got home.

About the same time, Kat got a visit from an Air Force officer mentioning that this was the end of her career. Kat had worked herself up from an airman to a major, and the Air Force was her whole life. She was seventeen years in and only three years away from full retirement. I remember it so vividly. The look of despair on her face.

"They are kicking me out?"

It was her whole life that had been pulled out from under her. It would take another year for the Air Force to officially retire Kat. God knows everyone fought hard to let her stay in. She could have worked from home her last couple of years, but in the end, it just wasn't feasible to be a wounded warrior on active duty in the Air Force.

CHAPTER 33

HELL AT NIGHT

THE DEMONS CAME AT NIGHT, FOR BOTH OF US. KAT WAS crying for help, crying for it to be a mistake, a bad dream she would wake up from.

To see Kat realize she is paralyzed from the neck down, to look into her eyes trying to explain that she cannot move, ever again. To explain that the Air Force will medically discharge her, that she will need 24/7 help with everything for the rest of her life. To explain that she will never have kids, never have sex like before, never ever walk again, much less run, go dancing, put on her makeup, pin up her hair, and hug anyone. How do you explain it to someone so active?

Death is easy.

Actually living and dealing with that amount of sadness, every day and night, slowly rips you apart from the inside out.

Every day we make it is a win. Back then, in the intensive care unit, and now, five years after the accident.

CHAPTER 34

MY TWO BEST FRIENDS

PAULINE, MY EX-WIFE, SAT NEXT TO MY HOSPITAL BED, CRYING. She was scared. I was the one in charge of the operational side of Fighterdiet, and I was out of commission. I knew she had the whole world on her shoulders, and I did what I could to calm her down.

"We will be fine," I said. "Let Vanesa run Fighterdiet, and you do your thing."

Vanesa was our second in charge at the time.

Pauline put her brave face on. She entertained the masses, her two million Facebook and Instagram fans, and she kept Fighterdiet going. She must have felt so alone. To this day, she is here, every morning, checking up on me. She never waivered.

Ted, a former UN soldier, parachuter, mountain climber, and my best friend since high school, heard about the accident via Facebook. He immediately told his boss, "You can fire me if you want, but I'm going to see Pavel."

He came from Sweden as fast as the transatlantic flight would allow and stayed for two months. He was always there, ready to catch me if I fell. Always in the background, watching. Five years up to today, he is still here for me. For now, he's bound to Sweden by the pandemic, but he's always available on messenger and Face-Time. He messages me every morning.

I was there for him when he went through a hard loss not long before the accident. We have been there for each other off and on our whole lives. The bonds you create when you are younger, when you have time to really spend time with each other, are special. That disappears as you get older. You never seem to have that much leisure time again.

When people saw me and Ted together, they always asked, "Are you brothers?" And I used to say, "Not by blood." Now when they ask, "Are you brothers?" I say, "YES." Family is who you choose to be your family, or maybe more accurately, who chooses you. I had Pauline and I had Ted. I had always had them, now more than ever.

Ted works as a motorcycle and gun instructor in the Swedish Army and at a rehab center for kids dealing with drug abuse. With over twenty years of experience working with people, his words to me, "You did nothing wrong," helped to set me on the right path.

CHAPTER 35

MORE SWEDISH FRIENDS

TED AND ERIK ARE MY TWO CHILDHOOD FRIENDS FROM Sweden. I was grateful to see their faces. They came when it was time for me to go home from the hospital after one week in the ICU.

My sister came too, also from Sweden. She stayed a short week. That's the last I have seen of my sister, five years and counting. Erik stayed a couple of days and flew back home fast. I never saw him after that either.

At my worst, when I was suicidal and in despair, I asked Erik to text me every morning so I could have someone to be accountable to, to not kill myself. That was too much to ask of him. He blocked me on Facebook, and we have not spoken since.

Erik did reach out via email about a year ago, stating, "I didn't even know why we argued," and asked if there was a possibility of re-connecting.

Let me first say this:

I was very bitter for not getting help, but now, five years later, I hold no ill will toward you, Erik. Many of my best and wildest memories are from our adventures together, like riding from Sweden to Ibiza on motorcycles!

You have to understand that for me, every day is the day of the accident. I wake up and brace myself for another day. Every day is a fight for decency for my wife, to see her smile and to get through the day. I am focused on being strong, mentally, emotionally, and physically, for her and me.

Back then, just after the accident, when I was home alone with Kat and she was screaming and crying, I had no one. I was begging on my knees for help. Back then, you let me go when I needed you the most, Erik.

If we meet now, what are we going to talk about? The weather? Our work? When I ask you about your child, will you ask me about my wife? Do you remember her? The last time you saw her, she was walking. Now she's paralyzed from the neck down, and you haven't asked about her once.

So I tell people who ask me. I have forgiven you and everyone else who did not help me when I asked you to, but I don't want to share my dinner table with you. I gave you the opportunity to be my hero, and you said no.

Ted, on the other hand, stayed for months. The definition of family and friends changed during this period in my life. Unwillingly, all relationships were tested, and some broke and some got forged in fire.

"Most people cannot deal with grief, their own mortality, or really be present to themselves and others. When you are truly awakened, it is largely a lonely path. I am grateful that you and your wife do have good and present people surrounding you. I understand the deep level of disappointment regarding family and friends you would think would be there, who are not. Sending you both love from my heart. Keep up the good fight—you have a strong message for us all."

Nikky Beast, one of my Facebook followers, was right. This was to be my own journey with the support of a few loyal warriors. To survive, I had to change the way I looked at the world. In time, maybe I could inspire others to push through when the devil comes knocking on the door.

CHAPTER 36

BACK HOME AND DAY DRINKING

I WAS RELEASED FROM THE HOSPITAL AFTER ONE WEEK IN THE intensive care unit, and I was left to figure out the rest for myself. The ambulance dropped me off with the monster halo screwed into my skull, a bottle of opioids for the pain, and a life in shambles.

Last time I had seen my home was leaving for a Christmas party. Kat and I had decorated for happy times, and seeing the Christmas tree again, I fell into the abyss. It was so sad seeing our home decorated for happy times, and it was now all just despair and hopelessness.

On the kitchen table, mail was stacked in a huge uneven pile. I panicked. I panicked because I was the guy who was always in control. I saw that unopened huge pile of mail and it just got to me. I was slowly understanding what this accident would mean for me, for Kat, and for our lives. To survive, we would have to change who we were as human beings. There was no room for perfectionism anymore.

Always-clean cars, bills paid on time, fingernails cut, all voice-mails answered. All that was out the door. Our new reality was chaos, on all levels. Seeing that huge pile of unopened and unevenly stacked mail was my first step in giving up and surrendering to chaos. There was no room for anything anymore. Only survival.

Three years later, a nurse asked me, "Doesn't anything bother you?" and I smiled. In the five years after the accident, I had only lost my temper twice, and both times were when Kat was mistreated. No, not much bothers me anymore. I practice being present today. I work on cherishing what I hold dear, every day, because I know what it's like to plan your whole life and have it taken from you.

The first night home, I stuffed myself with opioids, got help from Ted to climb into our rented hospital bed and tried to sleep. A howling wind woke me up in the middle of the night. It felt evil. The door in my room was open to the backyard, and I felt Kat's anger slamming the door. Was I hallucinating due to the opioids, or was Kat's spirit really there?

The first morning at home, I staggered out into the living room. Ted was half asleep on the couch, awake but silent. I knew he was there in case I fell, mentally or physically. I slowly made it to my standing desk and woke up the computer by touching the keyboard. I grabbed the mouse with my right hand. I couldn't move my fingers. I couldn't raise my fingers to click. I moved the mouse to my left hand and clumsily worked with my left hand instead. It would take weeks before the fingers on my right hand would start to obey my mind again. They were not paralyzed, but so much in my body was beat up and just would not work right.

I couldn't stand for very long. My broken neck and fractured skull took all my energy, so I worked in bursts. Twenty minutes on, sat down for thirty minutes, twenty minutes on, sat down for thirty minutes.

That first morning, I walked around the block with the help of my sister, and it took all I had. It was like running a marathon. The next morning, I walked two blocks, and I continued like that for months. I was not allowed to use any weights due to my broken neck, so walking became my exercise of choice. I was a fit muscular guy before the accident. However, my muscles slowly disappeared, but I kept my lungs and cardio going.

My work was with health and fitness, so I had a good understanding of what I needed to do to heal. I ate almost exclusively vegetables, berries, fruit, and lean protein. At night, I drank scotch, a lot of it, to be able to fall asleep, at least for an hour or two at a time. I was determined to heal up and heal up fast so I could help Kat. I figured it was better to get some sleep with the help of scotch than get no sleep.

It has taken me five years to occasionally get a good eight hours of sleep. I still have a scotch or two at night to calm my nerves and stop my brain from spinning. I don't day-drink. I only have those nightly ones to let myself relax and doze off.

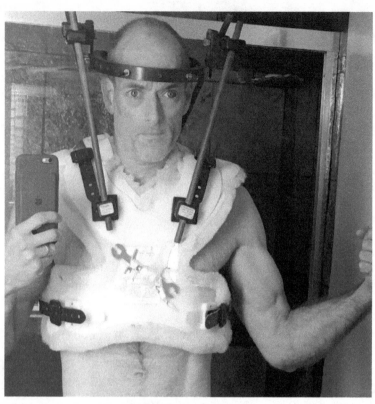

I looked at myself in the mirror that first morning at home.
Determined then. Determined now.

CHAPTER 37

THE ELEMENTS

My teeth were shaking, and my body was shivering. I was cold on purpose; it made me feel alive. The first week at home, I embraced all the elements. I soaked in the sun and I shivered on my morning walk. I walked out wearing nothing but a tank top or a T-shirt with the arms cut off to fit my halo.

We forget what is needed for life to prosper, but when you are near death, you revert to wanting only sun, air, and water.

I see it at the VA Spinal Cord Center where dozens of paraplegics and quadriplegics are sitting and laying outside with their faces turned toward the sun, just soaking it in. I see it in the homeless people, sleeping on the sand by the waterfront. I see it in myself. I have this pull to the water, and now nothing makes me happier than when I get to go to Belize and swim in the green, warm sea. It feels like home.

Universally, everyone seems to have that pull to the ocean, and it makes me wonder if that is where we all came from.

CHAPTER 38

WILL GOD WIPE HER ASS?

KAT AND HER MOM DID NOT HAVE A LOVING RELATIONSHIP early on in their lives. Most thought this was an excellent opportunity for Rosa to right all her wrongs and stay with me and take care of Kat, but she didn't want to. Rosa said she had to go home to Chicago to work, to her cleaning job at a hotel.

She said, "God will take care of my daughter."

I yelled at her, "Will God wipe her ass too? Will God turn her in bed? Will God feed her? I need help, for God's sake!"

Kat's brother threatened to beat me up for yelling at his mom. I welcomed him to it, well knowing that Ted stood right behind me and would defend me. I had the monster halo screwed into my skull and was in no condition to fight.

How hard must it be for Adam? His sister, lifeless in an American hospital, and his mom in tears.

I could understand his anger. The trauma made everyone angry and in need of justice. I brought a lot of pain into his life; I could see why he hated me. I understand why everyone needed someone to blame. How could this happen to wonderful, sweet, giving Kat? Kat, who accepted God as her savior. How could God allow this?

Someone must be to blame for this. I was the driver and the one easiest to blame.

I was desperate, and no one in either of our families wanted to help. No one was willing to do what I needed. I literally asked on my bare knees, but no one answered my screams for help.

I brought a lot of pain into everyone's lives, and that is what they wanted no part of.

Most work so hard every day to find a meaning in their lives. Horoscopes, Instagram, self-improvement courses, food, the gym. They work so hard to find happiness. What most missed was that this situation was offering them a way to be a hero. A way to be respected and to respect oneself. Here was the opportunity everyone was looking for in life but most didn't take it because it meant responsibility. No one wanted the responsibility and the work that came with the reward of being respected and a hero.

CHAPTER 39

EVERYDAY HEROES

WHAT MAKES A HERO? WHAT SPECIFIC QUALITIES MUST A hero have? Pauline formulated it for me in a text when she described Matt:

> They must unselfishly and unconditionally lay it all on the line for someone else. They must go above and beyond any rhyme or reason and sacrifice without ever expecting to be repaid.
> They would do this because their heart commands them to do so, not giving them any choice in the matter.

Kat and I have many such heroes in our life; that is why we still are alive.

MATT

An average Joe. A general contractor. American flag on the porch, drives a Jeep. Anyone and everyone.

Matt is married to Cherrie, and Cherrie and Star are sisters. They are both Belizean and grew up in Belize. Matt met Cherrie in Belize when he was a young building contractor down there.

Cherrie reached out to Kat on Facebook when she saw Kat was moving to California. Cherrie knew Kat because they shared a half-sister, Amileth; same father, different mothers. Rosa had Amileth adopted when she was two years old, and she grew up with her adoptive parents in southern Illinois.

In LA, Cherrie and Kat reconnected as familiar Belizeans.

After the accident, Matt's wife, Cherrie, immediately contacted Air Force First Sergeant Carlos Martinez, one of Kat's friends, to help get a hold of the Air Force. You see, Matt knew Kat would be AWOL (absent without leave) from work if they were not notified.

What Matt did for us was beyond the call of duty. He made himself the coordinator between the Air Force and me, the doctors and me, and everyone else and me. He protected me from everyone, and he protected Kat.

Matt drove me to and from the VA hospital more times than I can remember. He was there with us, always, for months until this day. It's hard to quantify his efforts in time or money, but I can say it felt like he was what I wanted my family to be like. Now he is family. **True love.**

CHAPTER 40

FUCK YOU!

I YELLED AT MATT. I SCREAMED, "FUCK YOU! WHY DIDN'T YOU tell me?"

Matt didn't flinch; he just continued walking down the hospital hallway beside me. He let me be mad. He let me fight him verbally for months and never waivered, never ever said anything back. He just absorbed it. We walked down the hospital hall. We lived in these faded cream-colored and gray hospital hallways. I don't even remember why I said "Fuck you" that time. I was in a rage from what was happening to my life.

My beloved Rolex watch. I had always wanted one. I had fought, bled, and saved, and after five years in America, I walked into a Rolex store and bought one outright with cash in hand. That was one of my proudest moments.

While I nowadays measure my success in friends and what I can do for others, back then, I wanted to show the world that I had made it, and that Rolex was that statement. The ones who have a Rolex know one when they see one, and that was the crowd I wanted to belong to.

Three months after the accident, I gave Matt my Rolex watch.

Cherisa, Matt's daughter, made a post on Facebook commenting that she would someday give her loving and supportive dad a

Rolex watch for being such a good dad, and I immediately knew what to do.

Little over a week later, I let Cherisa give her dad my Rolex. That is the only time Matt flinched a bit. After months of being a true hero, he looked bewildered and flabbergasted. I cried with Kat as we saluted our everyday hero.

Matt's daughter, Cherisa, and Matt at the dinner when we gave him the watch.

I later sent photos of me giving Matt my Rolex to Dr. Murphy. This Christian doctor knew everything about paying it forward, and somehow he finally got the watch he was saving up for.

I could tell Dr. Murphy was proud of me. It was one of the first steps of me changing my ways. Purging myself from my previous life to my new life. A new life of giving without expecting anything in return. A new life based on thinking of others first, just like Kat always does.

Matt, me, and the Rolex.

I am convinced these everyday heroes are the people who run into the World Trade Center to save people or excel in war zones or, as in our case, lend support for days, weeks, and years to come, always there, never wavering, never expecting or asking anything in return.

I saw and still see the most heroic behavior in regular people. It was never the Special Forces guy, or the accomplished business-man, or the athlete, or the fierce cage warrior. It was always the average Joe who stepped up and laid it all on the line for us. Why that is, I don't know. I just know that is how it was and is for us.

CHAPTER 41

TAKE CARE OF HER OR I WILL HUNT YOU DOWN

K AT WAS OUT OF IMMEDIATE LIFE-THREATENING DANGER, and now it was time for rehab and getting accustomed to a new life being paralyzed. So we were moved from Long Beach Hospital to a special VA spinal cord injury and rehabilitation unit.

I was saying my goodbyes at Long Beach Memorial Hospital as we prepared to move to the VA.

Dr. Murphy put all of his weight behind the words, "Take care of her or I will hunt you down."

At that point, I honestly didn't know what that meant, and if I had known, maybe I wouldn't have been so fast to answer, but I didn't want to let Dr. Murphy down, so I said I would.

Dr. Murphy had lived with paralysis in his family, and he knew what I was in for. He made me man up to the task. I had to be **strong for Kat**.

CHAPTER 42

THE VA

KAT WAS MOVED TO THE VA. THEY HAVE A SPECIAL CARE UNIT for spinal cord injuries. This was to become our home for the next three months. Some never leave. They come and they end up in the long-term wing.

A spinal cord injury is something the devil made up on one of his more innovative days. Not only can you not move, but you need catheters inserted every three hours, for life, to pee. You need help with bowel care. Every morning, someone has to insert an enema and use finger stimulation to assist a bowel movement. If not relieved, your blood pressure spikes, making you susceptible to a stroke.

You get neuropathic pain, an intense burning feeling in your limbs, like third-degree burns. Your body slowly disintegrates since you can't load it with activities. Muscles atrophy and bones get fragile and break. You get a bed sore because you spend too much time in bed on one side. It gets infected and you become septic and you die, or you die from the simple flu, since you cannot cough as the germs fester in your lungs so you develop pneumonia. If you somehow manage to survive this, your blood pressure will spike fast and hard. You will overheat because your body can't control its temperature, and then a stroke will kill you or make you brain dead. **Welcome to everyday paralysis, Kat's new life.**

This is why there is a special unit for spinal cord injuries. There is no end to the side effects. The paralysis itself is just the entrée. Then you have this full spectrum of daily side effects to deal with.

Kat was in her room. She had visitors, and I was there. One of the nurses said, "I'm glad you all are here. It's going to take a village." I didn't understand what she meant, but it became glaringly obvious once we got home. My insurance was maxed out after one week in the ICU, and Kat's Tricare insurance no longer covered any home care after she was medically retired.

How do you finance and organize 24/7 nurse care? How do you scrape together $132,000 a year to pay minimum wage to caregivers for Kat. Most organize a fundraiser for a $1,000 for their dog or cat or some other benefit close to their heart. We had to get $132,000 per year, every year, forever. After tax.

The VA doesn't cover 24/7 care. At most, they cover five to six hours of bowel and bladder care per day and four hours four times a week for home health aid. No wonder most thought Kat would end up in a nursing home.

CHAPTER 43

UBER AND DEMONS

I was told by my neurosurgeon, Dr. Nargess, that I would have the halo on for three months. I am six-foot-two, and with the halo on, I couldn't fit in any car but large SUVs. I could not turn my neck, so I couldn't drive. I was left to order an Uber SUV every day to go to see Kat. That is how I spent $5,000 on Uber, unwillingly, and it's how the money started pouring out of our savings account.

My days these first months became routine. Routine is the enemy of depression and demons. If you know what to do, it is much easier to get through the day. Wake up. Work two to three hours. Walk. Take an Uber to see Kat. Drink scotch. Try to sleep. That was my life for the three months while Kat was at the VA.

One of Kat's Air Force colleagues, Chris, had started coming over to the house. He came with groceries for me. No one asked him to; he just did it. I later found out Chris had spent time in the hospital too, all alone. His girlfriend told me that he respected me for taking care of Kat, and he wanted to do what he could to help me and Kat.

While I was overwhelmed trying to keep my company afloat and at the same time heal my body, Kat was stuck in a bed with her thoughts. Being paralyzed, you have all the time in the world to think about everything that you are missing out on. To think about why this happened to you.

CHAPTER 44

PEOPLE ANGELS

From day one at the VA, something magical happened. People showed up day and night, and Kat was never alone. This was when I truly started realizing what a remarkable woman she was. Her room was filled with friends and colleagues 24/7. People flew in nationwide and from abroad. For three months, she was never alone, not once.

Cherrie and Star and Kat's Air Force family pulled a big load. They spent a lot of days and nights at the VA, and the nurses at the VA had never seen anything like it. **True love.**

Four people came for me. Three flew in from Sweden—my sister and two of my best friends, Ted and Erik—and one was here, Pauline. I dare to say over a hundred came for Kat.

It was glaringly obvious where our priorities had been pre-accident. I thought I had friends, but I didn't. They were colleagues and peers, but they never showed up for me.

This accident tore our families apart and created a new one. **A family made by true love.**

CARLOS AND EDDIE

Carlos and Kat were stationed at Los Angeles Air Force Base together. Carlos was the one who got the news first. He was the one who notified Kat's superiors at the LA Air Force Base about the accident. Carlos had moved on to another assignment in Colorado and asked his friend, Eddie Monge, to take his place and be by Kat's side.

Eddie Monge is a big muscular guy with a heart of gold and always a jokester. He came to the VA and introduced himself, and he never left. Kat and Eddie found each other, and Eddie sat by Kat's bedside every day after work, talking about everything.

I think Eddie needed a female friend in his life, and Kat needed someone like Eddie who could make her laugh and talk about Air Force stuff. He made her feel a part of what was going on.

Today Eddie Monge is one of our best friends. **True love.**

Eddie Monge.

CHAPTER 45

WHY GOD, WHY?

FOR THE FIRST TIME IN MY LIFE, I WAS FORCED TO SLOW DOWN, to heal. I walked the beach listening to the entire works of the Joe Rogan podcast, Dr. Jordan's YouTube Channel, the Impact Theory podcast, Anthony Robbins, Dr. Joe Dispenza, the Rich Roll podcast, and numerous others. I had a mix of philosophers, doctors, and entrepreneurs in my ears, all day long. I needed answers as to why this had happened to us. Later, I also needed a financial plan for us. I knew I was living on borrowed time if I didn't make plans.

Today, I believe I would have had a village. After my accident, I had very few friends. The friends who visited at the hospital were the ones who really cared. When a man has a broken neck and you don't show up, you don't care. Out of the ones who did show up, several never came back to visit. My ex-wife, Pauline, and my childhood friend, Ted—those are my best friends. They are the only ones who really cared. Looking back, I am grateful I had two friends who had my back and still do.

I was very angry for a long time about the lack of support from the ones I thought were my friends. I felt abandoned. But it's deeper than that. The reckoning comes when you find out who has the inner strength to give support. They may like you, but it is more about their ability to provide support, not so much your situation. It is who they are in this life. They will react the same toward any crisis. They will withdraw and find excuses not to help or drop everything to be there for you.

CHAPTER 46

BLAME GAME

I was disappointed in my friends and family, and Kat was disappointed in me. I was in the process of healing my broken skull and helping Kat the best I could, but she pushed me hard with tasks to do for her, and when I physically could not move fast enough for her, she got angry. I felt that Kat wanted to punish me for what had happened to her. I was trying to heal so I could help her more later, but she wanted to test my willingness now.

I withdrew.

I was there every day, but I withdrew from her friends, her mom, her brother, her everything. All I felt was blame, their guilt toward me. Even if it was unspoken, it was always there. Even if they didn't mean it, it was there.

I didn't want to feel guilty, or I would never heal and I would break down mentally.

I had my reckoning with both heaven and hell the first week. Had it indeed been my fault, maybe hell would have taken me, but I knew in my heart that this was an accident. I had no control over it, and it may sound harsh, but that helped me. Knowing I was not at fault helped me push through and heal.

CHAPTER 47

NO MOBILITY

AFTER THREE MONTHS IN THE VA, THERE WAS A ROUTINE check to see how much mobility Kat had regained after the accident. Kat looked scared. I knew why. We both knew why.

A team of nurses and doctors poked her with a fork-like tool, and Kat was supposed to say something every time she felt it poke her, but she never said anything. This was just one more of those times where we sank deeper into the abyss. Any hope of regaining mobility or returning to a normal life was yet again denied to us.

I was slowly getting better. The halo had been on me for a couple of months, and some of my strength had started to return. But oh how I would sink back down into physical despair. Just wait, there is more, the puppet master said. I have so much more for you.

CHAPTER 48

THE PARASITES

WE ATTRACTED A LOT OF PEOPLE WHEN KAT WAS AT THE VA. They wanted to be part of the sympathy and the comradery that was shown all over Facebook.

They came as clowns, masked as caring for Kat. They came and sat by her bedside and became part of our growing group of supporters, but soon their true selves shone through their masks. Their intentions were not pure. They just wanted to be part of the attention. They promised to help. They promised to do whatever it took, but they did nothing.

I called out a couple of them, and they never returned. I wasn't subtle. I said, "If you promise something to Kat, you'd better keep it." They crawled back to where they came from, and we never heard from them again.

CHAPTER 49

THE WORLD GOES BLACK AGAIN

Two months after the accident, I still repeated, "I have to be strong for Kat," but I didn't have to actually verbalize it anymore. I just did it. It was who I was now. **I was strong for Kat.**

I pushed myself as hard as I could with the metal halo monster on my head. Two months after it was screwed into my skull, I was at my neurosurgeon's office for a checkup. I had X-rays done, and Dr. Nargess came in, looked at me, and said, "I have never seen anyone heal up as fast as you have. You get an A+ in healing!" Call it what you want, but I am convinced that repeating "I have to be strong for Kat" helped me to heal quickly. I was ordering my body to heal so I could help.

My bones had fused together naturally. My main injury was healed, but due to all my walking and body weight workout movements, the screws and the drill holes that attached the halo into my skull had gotten infected. Pus and blood were constantly around the drill holes.

Dr. Nargess said, "I will take the halo off one month early, but I need you to wear a neck brace for another two months." She didn't want to risk brain infection; that's why it came off.

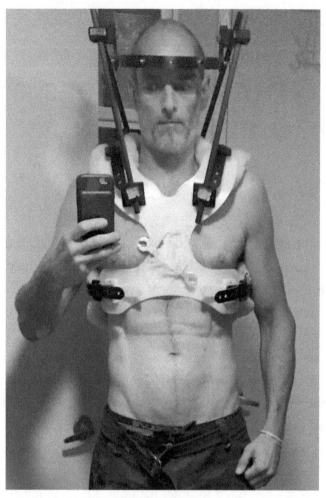

Two months of only walking. I had lost fifteen pounds of muscle,
but my mind was getting stronger.

The doctor called a technician, who came and unscrewed the Halo from my head. I got a neck brace, and they basically sent me on my way. Little did I know that only twenty minutes later, I would be back in the ICU with brain injury, a dislocated shoulder, a banged-up head, and in restraints on a gurney, because I was violent.

I walked out of the doctor's office feeling weak and having trouble thinking straight. I figured the trauma of taking off the halo was causing me to feel so weary. I walked to the outdoor coffee shop in the hospital atrium. I picked up an orange for some quick sugar and stood in line for an espresso. Once it was my turn, I said, "One espresso, please," but nothing came out of my mouth. Just a mumbling sound. The lady looked at me. I tried again. My mind said, "One espresso please," but my mouth said "mooooooooooooaaaaaaaaaaaa." Something was not right!

I clumsily pointed toward the espresso machine as I felt the sweat coming on. I got my espresso and started messaging my ex-wife. Kat didn't have her phone set up yet, so I couldn't message her.

In my head I typed in, "I need help, Pauline," but what came out in text was "#^&@%#@."

I panicked!

I could not speak and I could not text. I was locked inside my own head.

I used the recent call function and called Pauline and I heard her voice say, "Pavel," but I could only hear myself mumble back. It sounded like "mooooooooooooaaaaaaaaaaaa." Pauline must have sensed the urgency. She said, "Pavel, get help."

I have never been this scared in my entire life.

Was I condemned to live inside my own head for the rest of my life, not able to speak or write? I started walking back to the doctor's office, and just as with the car accident, my world went black. It was immediate. I was walking, and then nothing. I had passed out, stroked out right then and there, on the street.

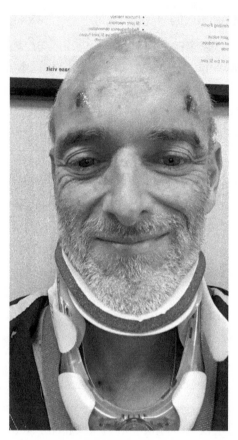

Me, just after the Halo came off. This was about twenty minutes before I lost my ability to speak or write and had a stroke.

I woke up in the emergency room, tried to talk, and could hear myself talk! I started to laugh and scream hysterically. Dr. Murphy looked at me with such a sad, bewildered face, but I was happy. I could talk again. I was okay. I WAS OKAY!

I had stroked out. When the halo was unscrewed, my head had been in a fixed position for so long, all my muscles had gotten weak and atrophied. The blood flow to my head was cut off when the head had to bear its own weight with no muscles supporting it, even with the neck brace on. I passed out on the street twenty minutes after the halo was taken off.

I was lucky. When I fell, I could have broken my neck again or died. I added another year of rehab due to the brain injury and dislocated shoulder I got from the stroke and the fall. Looking back, I am not sure how I survived that year. But again, the stroke was just life testing me for the real pain about to begin. If the physical pain couldn't kill me, maybe the mental pain would.

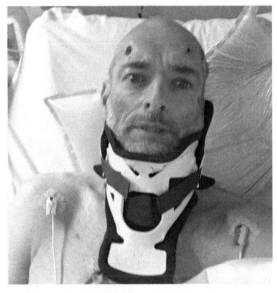

Back in the ICU after stroking out. I wanted to take a selfie to see what death looked like because that was how I felt. My dad said he saw that exact same stare in his father's eyes when he died.

CHAPTER 50

MORE DRUGS

THIS WAS A WEIRD TIME.

I was put on epilepsy drugs after my stroke. The drugs "slowed down" the activity in the brain to hinder more episodes. It's like living your life in slow motion. I was not allowed to drive for three months either.

The drugs made me dazed, and I didn't care about anything. I walked down to the beach and just sat there. It was a two-week period when I didn't even visit Kat at the VA. In all honesty, I enjoyed being dazed, not caring about anything. But I'm naturally a worker, and it wasn't for me to not do anything.

After two weeks, I told the doctor, "No drugs. It was like being a part of the walking dead. I would rather take my chances without drugs."

He gave me another drug and that one did not daze me as much. I was back.

CHAPTER 51

YOGA

My stroke set me back a lot. The halo was off my head, but now I had a dislocated shoulder to take care of. It would take a year to find out if I had permanent brain damage, and it would take a year to heal my dislocated shoulder too.

I walked into physical therapy with a neck brace, a shoulder brace, and a jacked-up, bloody right side of my face as that side of my body took most of the fall when I stroked out.

A statuesque athletic woman greeted me with a smile and did my initial evaluation. Almost immediately, I felt comfortable in her presence, and we both had a very relaxed attitude toward death and misfortune overall. Not that we don't care—quite the opposite. It's being able to talk about it that connects us. Most people are not, but we seem to thrive talking about it.

And isn't it so? You need to experience tragedy and sorrow to truly appreciate happiness and meaning, and we had both been down the path of darkness.

Over the months that followed, Heather and I became friends. She is into Buddhism and yoga, and one day she asked me, "Do you want to try?" The old me would have said no, but the new me said yes.

We rolled out yoga mats in the middle of her practice, and she held a yoga session, just for me, in the middle of the floor at her physical therapy practice. What just started was something that grew into something I am so proud of, even if my part was slim to none. Now Heather teaches yoga twice a week, for free, for anyone who wants to attend. **True love.**

Yoga made me whole again. I had the willpower myself, but yoga gave me the tools to put my body back together. It became an obsession the first two years, and my progress was fast and swift.

Heather and I are now, dare I say, best friends. I am forever grateful for her presence in my life, a true healer of human souls and bodies.

CHAPTER 52

MY BETRAYAL

AFTER THREE MONTHS AT THE VA, IT WAS TIME FOR KAT TO go home. The entire support staff from the VA and the Air Force was gathered around a big oval table. It was quite the sight. Doctors, physical therapists, psychologists, Air Force representatives—all were there. There must have been eight to ten people. It was time to do a final big meeting with the whole team and send Kat on her way.

I knew what I was in for. I had three months to think about it. I knew I had to betray Kat to help Kat.

Kat asked what would happen to her care once she got home as she needed 24/7 care.

"I don't want to be her caregiver," I told the support staff.

I knew Kat died inside when I said it, and I could tell she felt all alone. I was her last hope, and I'd let her down in front of all these people. I knew it would ruin the husband and wife part of our life. If you constantly shower and do enemas and catheters for your wife, she becomes your patient not your wife.

She still brings it up, and it still hurts, although I know she understands now. I had to heal up and take care of myself before I could help her. And truth be told, I wasn't ready to be a caregiver. I had started to change, but I wasn't there yet.

The VA promised there would be programs providing 24/7 care once the military insurance ran out. That was not true. Once Kat got discharged, we got around four and a half hours per day from the VA. The rest was up to us.

It took a long time, but one day I said, "It is an honor and a privilege to take care of you, Kat."

I had been given a chance to prove myself and help another human being, the one I love. **True love.**

CHAPTER 53

MY WISE DAD

TERJE, MY DAD, SAID IT BEST, "THE HOSPITAL IS EASY. YOU have 24/7 care. It is when you get home, it starts. You see, when you get home, you deal with subpar caregivers, death wishes, anxiety, and breakdowns."

He was right. He had taken care of his cancer-sick girlfriend for years while living deep in the Norwegian forest. He knew what it was like to be alone with the world on his shoulders with no one but himself to count on.

CHAPTER 54

PAY FOR
LIFE QUALITY

WHEN YOUR WIFE IS PARALYZED FROM THE NECK DOWN, HOW much is society willing to spend? Not much.

I see them all the time now. The ones committing suicide because they can't afford care for themselves or their loved ones. Sometimes they do it legally, sometimes not.

Sean, a Canadian man with ALS, was missing $263.50 a day for the last four hours of 24/7 care. He had twenty hours covered but needed twenty-four hours. He could not raise that money, and society would not give it to him. He chose euthanasia, which is legal in Canada. He chose death, and the price for his life was subsequently $263.50 per day.

Sean writes, "So left with the options of either waiting for a day that I have no staff available and choking to death, or being institutionalized at George Pearson (a VCH-run long-term care facility), the 'jail for quads,' and dying a slow torturous death, I'm going to pursue medically assisted death."

I did the math, and Kat and I have to fundraise, earn, and beg together $132,000. That is the cost for 24/7 care at minimum wage, per year. Care by caregivers, not nurses, just regular people we train to feed Kat, bathe Kat, do catheters, and do bowel care. Everything. Our price for Kat's life is $132,000 per year for the rest of our lives. The thought of that alone is enough to make you go crazy and give up.

I maxed out my insurance after one week in the ICU, after I reached the $100,000 threshold. Then I was dropped by Aetna. So there was nothing more to get there.

Kat's bill for the first year totaled nearly three million dollars. The 24/7 care via official nurse agencies is outrageously expensive. That was all covered by her military insurance. But there came a day when Kat would be medically retired, and we would not have that anymore. One day we had 24/7 care, and the next day we had none.

I stood there. Alone with Kat. It was her and I.

Welcome to financial hell.

CHAPTER 55

YEAR ONE HOMECOMING

So eventually, Kat came home. We lived in a beautiful but small apartment overlooking the ocean. Perfect for a young couple with careers, only home to sleep and entertain. Absolutely terrible for a person paralyzed from her neck down and one person with a dislocated shoulder, brain injury, and broken neck.

We had some security in knowing that Kat was still an active duty Air Force officer and her insurance provided 24/7 nurse care.

Most caregivers sent to us by the caregiver agency were subpar and had to be sent home though. I found myself googling "urethra" in the middle of the night to teach the nurses where Kat's urethra was. My wife with her legs spread wide open every three hours and a stranger clumsily inserting a catheter in the vagina instead of the urethra was killing me every time. The humiliation for Kat, the clumsiness of the caregiver, the situation in itself was impossible and inhumane.

The caregiver agency sent us nurses who were used to handling babies or older people. Kat was a young brilliant woman used to commanding her own troops and multimillion dollar projects. Obviously, she clashed with a lot of nurses and still does.

A paralyzed person needs help with everything. Absolutely everything. It's not just feeding, catheters, and bowel care. It's scratch my nose, turn the paper in the book, answer the phone call, turn up the heat, turn down the heat, move my hair, scratch my nose again.

Literally hundreds if not thousands of "little things" that we ourselves do every day without thinking about it. All these little things Kat has to ask someone to do. Every day. If you are not careful, it can sound like she nags, but she just needs help. If you hesitate, just for a millisecond, she feels like a burden. Kat, in turn, must brace herself every time she asks or even saves her asks for the times she really needs it just for the sake of not wearing us out. Kat hates bothering people. She prefers to be alone. Having to ask for help all the time gets her into depression at times.

We are two people running around like chickens to keep Kat alive and occupied. A caregiver and me. Kat is not a child. She is a retired US Air Force major, a woman who commands respect. She must be sitting up straight with her feet close together and facing forward. She gets annoyed when caregivers put her shirt on with the sleeves twisted, not centered on her body and not pulled down all the way. Her pants also need to be the same length at the bottom with the seams on the sides of her legs. Too often, the caregivers don't pay attention to those details, and it makes Kat a bit short tempered. How could they let her go out with ashy ankles? With sleep boogers in her eyes? Kat often demanded attention to detail, but sometimes it was just too much to ask.

We are taking care of a fully functioning human being with as many needs as you or me. She just cannot move her arms or legs.

We have to be her arms and legs.

CHAPTER 56

NURSING HOME

THE FIRST WEEK HOME, KAT DIDN'T DO MUCH; SHE COULDN'T do much. She was sitting in a sling by the window looking for the sun. Her Belize upbringing was so ingrained in her that she looked for the sun wherever she was and delighted in the warmth of the rays caressing her.

That day, the sun would not help her. It was another do-or-die day. We had lots of those.

Kat's head was bowed down, tears rolling down her cheeks, and I asked her, "What's wrong, babe?"

A friend of ours had written a letter to her fearing that she ultimately would end up in a nursing home due to the high cost of taking care of quadriplegics. He wasn't wrong; he was just insensitive.

Kat looked up at me, so sad, so heartbroken, and said, "Don't let me end up in a nursing home."

That was one of two defining moments for me. Right then and there I decided I would never let that happen. I would rob a bank before I'd let that happen. I meant it and I still mean it.

Today, more than five years after the accident and four years after that letter came, she told me, "I can live on one meal a day but no nursing home."

I reassured her that a nursing home would never ever happen.

Kat in her sling, staring out our window.

I had some time before the Air Force insurance would drop their 24/7 caregiver coverage, so I started making plans. Since then, I have not been to Starbucks more than a handful of times. I have sold all my belongings, absolutely everything. I have fundraised hundreds of thousands of dollars, and I have learned how to make money grow in the stock market.

CHAPTER 57

I MADE A DEAL WITH THE DEVIL

WE HAD BEEN HOME FOR A WHILE NOW, BUT EVERYTHING WAS different. Every morning, in the first seconds after waking up, I expected my wife to have her arm stretched out over me, holding me in her sleep. I expected to wrangle myself out of her grip, look at her, smile, and sneak out to make coffee. My white picket fence life, my happy life.

Reality hits me like an icepick. Bam! Bam! Bam! Intense sharp pain, right in the gut. The line between life and death is a real thing at 4:00 a.m. That's when the devil lures in the darkness of your mind. I remember my life, and I gasp for air. I brace myself for another day of war. I call it war because I have to mobilize every cell of my body to start a new day.

For me, this was the moment of truth. The day I wouldn't get out of bed, the demons had won.

I gave myself three seconds to get up. Never think, just do. It is still my mantra for life. When all else fails, doing will save you, just the sheer act of physically acting means you are moving forward. Sitting still and thinking just lets your brain rewind and replay all the bad parts. Doing forms new connections, new memories, new and better pathways to replay in your brain.

I peeked into the room next door where the night nurse sat in a chair next to Kat. Hopefully Kat was sleeping. Sleep is hard to come by for her, and we all pray for her to get more of it.

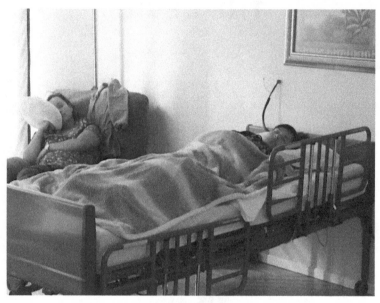

Cynthia, one of the caregivers who stayed with us the longest,
over two years, watches over Kat.

CHAPTER 58

WHAT IF NO ONE KNOWS AND WHAT IF YOU ARE ALL ALONE?

THE MOST TERRIFYING MOMENT I HAD AFTER THE ACCIDENT was not that my wife was paralyzed. It was not the halo screwed directly into my skull. It was not having a stroke in the middle of the street after losing my ability to speak or write.

It was the realization of being all alone.

It was the realization that no one knew what to do.

Not doctors, not psychologists, not priests. They were all just waiting for what they knew would be the end—for us to fail and perish. I asked them all point blank, "What would you do in Kat's shoes? In my shoes?" and they all looked away.

No one from Kat's side was there to help. No one from my side was there to help me. No family. Just me, in a halo. Broken. And my wife, paralyzed from the neck down.

How do you deal with the fact that you are the only one responsible for your wife, and you feel stuck? You can't divorce, travel, have fun, nothing. It may seem egocentric, but all those thoughts come at you like a ton of bricks, and you just want to run! Run away from all the responsibilities.

This is your life now, and you have no idea how to handle it.

Everything is easy in the hospital. You have 24/7 constant care and comfort. Even patients who are dying are looked after—especially if you are dying. You are juiced up with as many painkillers as you want. Palliative care is all about comfort. At home, it is just you, alone and forgotten. Well, not forgotten really, people just choose not to see you. They want their white picket fence lives intact.

There was always an excuse. My sister even said, "The accident was not my fault."

Kat's mom would rather work as a cleaning lady in Chicago than come and help me take care of Kat. My best friend, Erik, blocked me on Facebook when I asked him to text me every morning just so I had someone to be accountable to and not kill myself. Most of my industry friends chose to forget about me too.

If I sound bitter, it is because I was. I needed help. I begged on my knees for help.

Help would come, but it would take time.

The three-year hump. That is when many welcome the abyss. Three years of fighting. and then they've had enough. We were in the beginning of the storm. We were in year one. Our journey had just begun.

CHAPTER 59

ALONE

PEOPLE ASSUMED WE WERE OKAY BECAUSE WE WERE HOME.
It was quite the opposite.

Ted had left to go back home to Sweden. I needed all the help
I could get to take care of Kat at home and to heal myself at the
same time.

My sister was taking a trip from Sweden to Cabo, Mexico, close
to California. I asked her to please spend a few hours in Los Angeles. I told her I would pay for it. It would make Kat so happy. She
said no.

I asked my mom to come over from Sweden to help with dishes,
errands, whatever she could do. She used her age as an excuse
and never came. My dad offered money to have Ted stay with me
longer but couldn't come.

No one came.

It was me and Kat. Welcome to hell.

My worldview collapsed. I had spent hundreds of thousands of
dollars of my hard-earned money on trips for my mom and sister
to come to America, to vacation and have fun. I had gone out of
my way to stay connected with them and share my money with
them. In the end, that meant nothing.

When one of Kat's friends gave $1,000 instead of visiting, it became really clear to me that no one wanted any part of the sadness we brought into their lives. No one wanted their worldview changed.

It became clear why dogs, when they are badly hurt, crawl away to die alone. It became clear why infected ants are led away by guardian ants. Ingrained in nature, there seems to be an instinct to discard the weak and dying. As humans, you would think we would have evolved, but that is not always the case.

We were left to perish, and most thought we would. I didn't know it then, but everyone thought I would leave Kat and that Kat would end up in a nursing home, which would mean death for her.

Everyone wanted the easy way out for themselves. That's why they thought I would leave her. But I didn't.

* * *

I am paraphrasing Dr. Jordan Peterson, but the essence of his words is, "If you are suffering, and you can't bear life, take on what you can bear. Look a month ahead. If that is too much, look a week ahead. If that is too much, look at a day, a minute, a second."

And that's what I did. I took it second by second. Today, five years later, I am up to a day. I take it day by day.

That is probably how I should have lived all along, day by day. The present is everything.

Eckhart Tolle, the modern-day philosopher, says, "Life is now. There was never a time when your life was not now, nor will there ever be."

What he means is that you cannot go back in time, and you will never experience the future. You can only experience right now.

CHAPTER 60

ABUSE

KAT HAD BEEN ABANDONED AND TAKEN ADVANTAGE OF HER whole life. Abused, beaten savagely by her mom, and sexually abused by her mom's boyfriends at an early age.

I believe the search for safety, acceptance, and family is what brought us together, as I was on the same quest for a home and safety. I believe us lying on the couch holding each other tight in Las Vegas was and is the foundation of our love. We felt safe. We felt home. We felt loved.

When the accident happened, the whole world came to see us, but already, after one week at home, people dropped off. Kat's mom came to visit from time to time, but she blamed me for the accident. She didn't want to stay and help me take care of Kat.

Kat was heartbroken. When she needed her mom the most, she once again abandoned Kat.

All Kat had was me, and the realization that I was all she had was terrifying for me and, I am sure, for her. At some level, she still blamed me for the accident. For Kat to have me as her only family member taking care of her must have been pure hell.

CHAPTER 61

MOM AND SIS

I ASKED YOU BOTH FOR HELP, BUT I NEVER GOT IT. I DON'T know what to talk to you about now. What is there to talk about, Mom? What is there to talk about, sis? You are both forgiven, but I have nothing to say.

You both chose not to share the burden with me. My life revolves around Kat. If you are not willing to help me, there is nothing to talk about that won't just be trivial nonsense.

Anyone who wants to be part of my life is automatically part of Kat's life. That means helping out in whatever way you can, even if it is just a visit like I asked for, sis, or helping to do house chores for a week or two, Mom.

I waited for you both. I waited for you to fight for me. I waited for you to come over to America. I waited for you to watch the movies I sent you so you would understand my situation. I gave you the chance to be heroes and a real family forged in fire, but you never came.

I am not mad. I don't blame you anymore. I wish you all the best in life, I really do.

CHAPTER 62

GROWTH

It is ultimately my own fault. I measured myself in money and status. I should have measured myself in self-respect, empathy, and kindness. I've been given a second chance, and I've found true friendship, forged in fire.

When your wife wants to kill herself, and you consider suicide options, you wonder how you will make it through the next hour. Then it all matters. It really fucking matters who is there for you!

To this day, my best friends, Ted and Pauline, and my dad, Terje, check in with me every morning. They never fail. Not once have they failed, five years and counting.

Terje did come over to America during the second year, and he was very helpful. He is a very empathetic man with an ability to see others like only an artist can. He saw me. He saw my pain and my fight. He found the words to help. He knew he couldn't be there for me in person, as he had his life in Norway, but he emptied his nest egg for us, and he texts me daily.

Eddie Monge and Chris Beersingh are family now. They were Air Force colleagues of Kat who transcended that line between work and friends and became family.

Chris, me, Eddie Monge, and Detra.
Cuban night at Havana Mania Restaurant in Redondo Beach, California.

CHAPTER 63

FACEBOOK AND DETRA

Once I got home from the hospital, I started writing. I started posting on Facebook every day. I was brutally honest, and the pain resonated with many. I quickly gained a following. It was very unlike me to be so straightforward. I shared all my deepest inner thoughts with no filter whatsoever. In the beginning, there was a lot of anger. How could this happen? Why did this happen? It soon changed to disappointment, bitterness, and sadness.

Pressure?

If I die, there is no one.

No one to take care of Kat.

No one.

The pain is worse. She spasms harder. The neuro pain is like open wounds constantly burning.

I position Kat's head on my chest and we cry together.

I tell her to hang in there for my sake and for Chapo's.

I am asking her to live in constant pain.

Lifetime cost for a quadriplegic, forty years old, is three million dollars.

That's $100,000 for thirty years.

I WILL REST WHEN I DIE.

I screamed out on Facebook, and Detra heard me. She heard my despair. She recognized the pain she herself had gone through.

Detra had fought for her daughter's life. Jo-Jo was born with hemiplegia (paralysis) as a result of cerebral palsy from a brain bleed in her right hemisphere.

Doctors told Detra to end Jo-Jo's life because it would be too much for her to bear. Detra was still young, beautiful, and had a full life ahead of her. Jo-Jo would need lifelong care.

Detra's own family wanted no part of it. But Detra didn't see the paralysis. She saw her child, and she felt love. **True love.**

Detra heard me scream on Facebook. She reached out to me and shared her story. She listened to ours. She visited us, and she helped out as much as she could. We became friends. Close friends. Family.

CHAPTER 64

NEW FAMILY TIES AND I AM CHANGING

A YEAR AFTER WE MET DETRA, SHE TOLD KAT SHE WOULD have to sleep in her car soon. She was broke and getting evicted out of her house. She had no one to help and no funds to hire movers. She was in real despair.

Kat called Chris and Ted, who were here visiting us from Sweden. We all went over to Detra's place. What met us was sheer and utter chaos; it was a war zone. Detra was at the brink of losing it. Her daughter, Jo-Jo, sat in her adaptive chair in the middle of it all, in the midst of bags, cardboard boxes, clothing, and trash.

We looked at each other, and we all knew we had to get her out of that mess. Kat took charge! Chris and Ted, both military men, helped get Detra's belongings organized to put in a truck and storage. We spent all day cleaning out her house. Kat paid for it all.

Detra's two teenage boys were unable to do anything without being told what to do, probably in disbelief that this was happening to them. Detra and the boys moved in with us for a little while until she could get her bearings back.

Today, Detra lives in the outskirts of Los Angeles in a safe, green environment. Her daughter and her boys are thriving. Detra came to us when we needed everyone and had no one, and she became our someone. A year later, we got to repay her. If this is not the meaning of life and love, what is? **True love.**

* * *

I reached out to Detra when writing the book, and she sent these words and a photo of Jo-Jo:

> We miss both you and Kat. I am forever grateful toward you both. I was completely burnt out from being a caregiver, mom, and full-time employee. I am now in the country centered around nature, slower pace, and peace. I am completely focused on my own health, my sons are excelling in college during the pandemic, and I'm meeting Jo-Jo's daily needs.
>
> I felt your pain, Pavel. I knew what it was like to feel hopeless, and in my case, to have no one. Through you and Kat, I met my tribe, family. You both showed me and taught me the true meaning of unconditional love. You included not only me but also Jo-Jo which I am forever grateful for.
>
> You have such a huge heart to even think of us. You and Kat are angels on this planet. You both healed me.
>
> Detra.

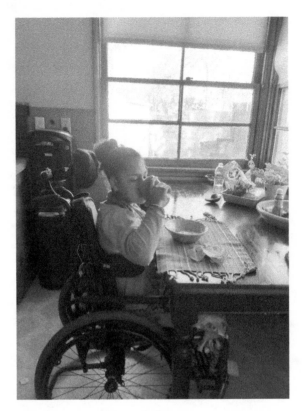

Jo-Jo.

CHAPTER 65

WE ARE
HANDICAPPED

WE HAD FOUGHT OURSELVES BACK FROM THE ABYSS, BUT FOR what? It wasn't the physical pain. It was not feeling normal that haunted us. We were "them" now. We were the ones people look at thinking, "I'm glad that's not me." We were one of those accidents you hear about on the news, except we didn't even make the news.

Every day that first year was filled with roller-coaster emotions. Every day, we discovered more things to make us sad. What kills me inside is not our physical damage; it is how people look at Kat. They judge, they look, and they look away.

When we finally got home and got our handicap-accessible van, Kat and I went grocery shopping for the first time. Pushing my wife in the parking lot on my way into the grocery store, I had a big knot in my stomach. We were "them" now. We were "the others, the outcasts, the handicapped."

People looked, and even worse, they did their best not to look while looking, which made it so much worse.

There is nothing easy about navigating a grocery store with a wheelchair, all while trying to make it seem normal. It is not normal. You bump into things, there is nowhere to keep the groceries. Kat cannot see above waist level. It's a cluster fuck of emotions and hell, just to get groceries.

Both Kat and I kept it together. But that first trip was pure hell.

AN ORIGAMI

WE DIDN'T MAKE MUCH OUT OF IT AT FIRST. SOMEONE SENT us an origami. A crane folded by hand, made out of paper. In time, more kept coming. One by one, sometimes several bound together.

Origami.

YEARNING FOR TOUCH

Sex, hugs, touch. You take it for granted when it is there, just like mobility.

Kat cannot reach out to hug me. She can't show affection. I think that is the most heartbreaking of it all. Often, I lay in bed with her, push my head up against her neck, and keep one hand on her shoulder so I touch her on the places she can feel me, so we can recharge our love. Touch and feel are literally the glue that holds us together. I think that goes for the whole human race. We need to feel like we belong, and we need social interaction. We need someone to yearn for us, to touch us.

This is how I choose to see Kat. It's how I see her in the past, today, and future. I don't see her paralysis. I see her dancing on a catamaran in Belize.

CHAPTER 68

NEVER ALONE

A SPINAL CORD INJURY WILL NEVER LET YOU OFF THE HOOK, it will only test you more.

No privacy, no peace of mind, no rest. The only time I am alone is when I shower and go to the restroom, and even then, the caregivers often walk in on me by mistake. I am grateful we have them because I wouldn't make it without them, but there is no privacy whatsoever. In a way, it's like living in a prison cell, on top of each other, constantly.

And Kat, poor thing, she never gets to be alone. Sometimes she pretends to sleep just to be alone. I know when she is pretending, and I tell the caregivers to let her be. Kat is condemned to a life with constant surveillance. She was a very private person before the accident, and now a caregiver has to do a catheter every three hours and bowel care every morning to get the stool out. It is heartbreaking, and she hates it.

When asked what they would rather have, the ability to have an erection or the ability to go to the restroom like a normal person, 100 percent of the men say the ability to go to the restroom. Bowel care is so degrading, and it has to be done every day.

CHAPTER 69

CHRIS

CHRIS WAS ONE OF KAT'S COWORKERS. HE CAME TO VISIT HIS fellow Air Force comrade, and just like Eddie Monge, he was there for the long run. He came back, over and over, to visit Kat. They slowly bonded.

Chris tried to reach out to me at the VA, but I wasn't in a good place. I was in severe physical pain due to the halo, and I was trying to save my business from going under.

Our first year at home was chaotic. Both Kat and I were trying to navigate our new lives. Both of us were in so much mental pain. I vividly remember Kat and I screaming at each other. Angry at each other and the world when Chris came by. He knocked on our door and walked in. I told him to get the fuck out. "Get out!" While Kat said, "No, stay!"

Chris just looked at us and slowly closed the door, but he didn't leave. He waited outside the front door. A half hour later, we let him in. I don't remember if I apologized, but I remember us being close friends ever since. You see, he fought for us. He understood it was our pain talking, not our hearts. I am forever grateful for the ones who saw past our pain and stuck it out with us.

Chris is one of our best friends now. He comes over to our house almost every day, and it is literally friendship forged in fire. He did what you would expect a family to do. **True love.**

CHAPTER 70

CAN SHE MOVE YET?

PEOPLE MEAN WELL WHEN THEY ASK, "HOW'S KAT?" WHAT they really mean is, "Can she move yet?"

The first years, I said, "It's still early. Mobility can come back anytime." Phrases like that. I later realized I only said that to make the person asking feel good.

The reality is that there is slim to no chance to regain mobility. Most paralyzed persons who recover have the advantage of being able to move "something." If you can't move anything, you can't work the muscles, and the mind–body connection is not there. It's all the luck of the draw, and we were not lucky. At least not yet.

Kat's spinal cord is bruised and damaged, and it has atrophied. Nerves do grow back, but the amount of nerves that would have to regenerate and the time it would take makes it very unlikely for Kat to ever move again. They say the body heals a millimeter a day on a cellular level, so time may be on our side if we live that long and her muscles are still functional.

Nowadays I answer like this, "We have more good days than bad days. Today was a good day." Or, I remind the person asking how Kat fought herself off the ventilator and her feeding tube, being able to breathe on her own and eat real food through her mouth.

If Kat wasn't a warrior, she would have been bedridden and on a ventilator that was breathing for her, unable to speak, for life.

Remember, I tell them! When Kat woke up from her coma-like state, with the ventilator tube inserted in her windpipe, it made it impossible for her to talk. All we had was eye contact. Kat could not move and she could not talk. She could not breathe on her own and she could not eat solid food. That was her starting point, and look at her now! Kat has come so far.

What a sight we were. Me in a halo and Kat totally destroyed. Just two young kids really. Two kids brought together in search of safety and love, and here we were, shells of our former selves. But we are still alive, making sure the other one is as well taken care of as possible. Love will make you do that. **True love** will make you do that.

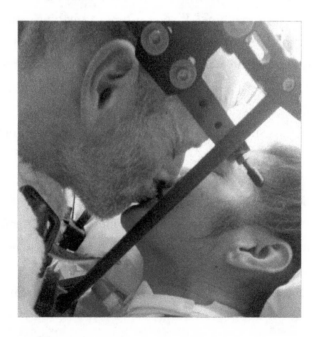

CHAPTER 71

REMEMBER THE ORIGAMI

ONE DAY A HUGE BOX CAME. IT CONTAINED A BOOK AND A thousand paper cranes. I remember opening it up in disbelief. Penny Haspil had made them all by hand. There was a book and a note.

Kat,

This book is a sad story, but I find it special for the young characters' courage and outlook and her classmates' goodwill. It also explains why I would fold and send a thousand paper cranes, sort of.

I think it has been my form of prayer for you. I still believe a miracle breakthrough is just around the corner. Best of hopes & hugs to you!

Penny

I just stood there and looked at one thousand hand-folded paper cranes and, in my hand, the book *Sadako and the Thousand Paper Cranes* by Eleanor Coerr.

It is just one example of how Kat has touched hundreds if not thousands of lives. Kat makes other people better human beings.

CHAPTER 72

STUCK FOR LIFE?

We screamed a lot at each other the first year.

It wasn't just the injuries. Everything changed the first year. How much time do you really spend with your spouse? An hour a day, thirty minutes, a little time after work, or is it just you two in bed together watching Netflix? Is that your quality time?

All of a sudden, Kat and I went from seeing each other briefly in the morning and an hour after work to being together, all the time. 24/7. Now is when I really found out who I married. We had never spent this much time together ever, and now we got to do it when Kat was paralyzed and I had a halo on my head.

I felt Kat's anger. I felt her pushing me away because of what had happened to her. I think she understood it was an accident, but emotionally, she was lashing out, and I was an easy target. I was willing to take it just because of her situation. It was a bad year, this first year. It was a really bad year.

I knew I had to get strong fast and I knew I had to take care of myself first, so I could later be there for her. Kat never acknowledged that, and none of our friends did either. Or maybe they did, but I wasn't able to see it. I was alone in my battle to get well. I don't blame Kat, and I don't blame them. Kat was and is paralyzed from the neck down.

I was okay in comparison, but I still had to overcome the halo, the stroke, dislocated shoulders, brain damage, and mental issues. I found my healing powers in the podcasts I listened to and the encouraging responses on my Facebook posts.

"Pavel! You are my hero! I can't believe you could do this with the HELL you've been through. MY TEN-YEAR-OLD SON DIED in a terrible CAR ACCIDENT only a few weeks before your accident. I have been following you and Katherine Portillo because your STRENGTH helps me keep going."

—RACHYMAMA

"I love your soul. Your love for Kat, your strength to overcome pain and darkness, your day-to-day battles, they're all so inspirational."

—ANONYMOUS

"I watch both of you (Kat and Pavel) in awe every day via Facebook. You've met this unfair life challenge with such grace and fortitude… you are an inspiration to many, myself included."

—JEFF O'CONNELL (CHIEF EDITOR OF BODYBUILDING.COM)

CHAPTER 73

BULLET OR CANCER

EVEN WITH 24/7 CAREGIVERS, IT WAS NOT ENOUGH. THEY work grueling twelve-hour shifts, and they are never as fast as Kat wants them to be. They're often on their phones, not paying attention to Kat.

We were in fight or flight mode all the time. We were trying to accommodate life at home. Nurses came and went, my business was slowly going down the drain, and poor Kat was sitting by the window looking out at the boardwalk where she used to run, cycle, and live.

I was convinced of death that first year. Not dying wasn't even a consideration. It was just a matter of what would get me first— an imaginary bullet to my head, or that constant ache I had in my stomach. Stress-related cancer or another stroke was what I thought would kill me. I was high strung 24/7.

Frank, our Filipino landlord, was an architect. He owned the duplex we lived in. He lived above and we rented the apartment below.

It is surely an island trait, caring and looking out for your loved ones and your neighbors. Without even asking, he suggested widening the doors so Kat's wheelchair could pass by the doorways. He contacted the city to arrange for a handicap spot outside his building. He built a concrete ramp for Kat's wheelchair to get into the house. Such a wonderful warm soul, our Frank. **True love.**

CHAPTER 74

NEXTSTEP

ME IN A HALO AND KAT IN A WHEELCHAIR. WE WERE BROKEN and felt like outcasts. There are very limited resources available once you leave the hospital. The VA provides rehab, but in all honesty, it is a sad place where most seem to go for coffee and social time, not to really try to get better. While my healing slowly progressed via light-strength training, yoga, and walking, Kat had nothing.

We had heard great things about a rehab facility called Next-Step. If NextStep was anything like the VA rehab center, it was just another place to die. Opening the door to NextStep, we were met by blasting music, and one of the jacked trainers yelled, "Welcome!" The trainer came up to us and introduced himself. "I'm Joel." He didn't say he was a triathlete, but he was and he looked the part. Tall, lean, buff. I said, "Go easy on Kat." He said, "If she passes out, she passes out," and I immediately fell in love with this place and the trainers here.

This was a place filled with tough love. Tears allowed, but get right back at it. This was *SISU*! It had its founder's spirit engraved in every team member. *SISU* is Finish and translates to something like "fight and never give up despite overwhelming odds." Janne Kouri was the founder, a warrior paralyzed in an accident just like

Kat. He was there every day, fighting for himself and for others to have a chance, to have hope and to feel normal.

Kat and Joel.

CHAPTER 75

CAREGIVER DRIVES INTO THE WALL

WE LIVED ON A STEEP HILL OVERLOOKING THE OCEAN, SO getting in and out of the handicap-accessible van was a real challenge. The car was always parked facing down the hill. You would turn the wheels max left, slowly accelerate, straighten the wheels, and drive with one foot on the brakes down to the busy crossroad just below. It was a little bit of a maneuver, and we had to do practice runs with new caregivers to check that they knew how to do it.

This particular morning, Kat was in a hurry to get to her appointment at NextStep. She was in a hurry every morning, so this was nothing new. The caregiver was new though. She wheeled Kat into the van. I kissed Kat goodbye and started walking up the hill where my car was parked. I was on my phone, still walking up the hill, when I heard a terribly familiar sound!

BOOM!

I still remember it in my bones. I turned around in slow motion and it took a second for me to register the unimaginable. The nurse had driven full speed into the neighbor's house, straight into a brick wall! Instead of pumping the brakes lightly the nurse had pumped the gas, panicked, and swerved into the house's wall to avoid crossing the busy intersection below.

I sprinted downhill while calling Matt. I knew I needed help. Matt is always the first person who comes to mind when these things happen. He is cool under pressure and always has a solution.

I reached the van. I tried to open the passenger door. It was stuck. I yelled, "Kat, Kat." I started kicking the door with full force. Frank, our godsent landlord, came out from his house and asked how to help. I yelled, "Call 911."

I tried the front door again and somehow got it open. On the floor, under the steering wheel, the nurse was hunched in a fetal position, shaking, and screaming uncontrollably. All air bags had deployed. She was alive but in shock.

I looked back toward Kat. I should have known. She had kept her cool.

"Siri, call 911."

Kat was hanging halfway out of her wheelchair trying to call 911, but Siri wasn't listening. The phone was too far away from her. I reached in to straighten Kat up and get her out, but the wheelchair was stuck in its locking mechanism that was bolted to the floor. I couldn't get her out.

It was a hellish repeat of our first accident. While I was trying to get Kat's wheelchair unstuck from its locking mechanism on the van's floor, I was still in disbelief that this was actually happening to us.

I heard sirens in the distance, and I ran to meet the ambulance and the fire rescue. Next, I am swarmed with help, Kat is put on a gurney, and we are off in an ambulance to the emergency room.

We never saw that caregiver again. We had words with the care agency that provided her, but I am not allowed to write more about that.

Life was cruel. After being paralyzed in a car accident, Kat was now in another car accident. After X-rays, Kat was given the all-clear to go home.

I still kept it together, but I would soon break.

At the hospital, Matt leaned in toward me and asked, "How are you doing?" and I know he knew I wasn't all there. He looked at me and said, "If anyone can do it, you can!"

I didn't answer him because I wasn't so sure anymore. We all have a limit, and mine was about to show its ugly face.

Pictures from the actual incident.

CHAPTER 76

FOR BETTER OR FOR WORSE IN REAL LIFE

THIS IS WHAT PEOPLE ASK THE MOST: "HOW LONG HAD YOU been married when the accident happened?"

I never understood the question until Kat one night told me, "I had one year of bliss. That is all I got." I don't think she meant one year of marriage, I think she meant one year in her whole life.

WE FALL INTO THE ABYSS

We met them at the same time, Kat and I, our demons. I knew Kat was suicidal, or at least, I thought she was. Kat is so smart that if she wanted to kill herself, she would figure out a way, even if she could not move her hands or feet. This was a big concern of mine, and I tried to stay one step ahead of her, thinking of ways she could do it.

I even said, "If you decide to kill yourself, don't drive the wheelchair into traffic and let other people suffer. Find another way to do it." This may seem macabre to you, but this is the mental state we were in. It was literally life or death, day by day.

Kat was on her standing frame, a contraption that straps her in and lets her stand up. It's good for her blood pressure and loads her bones using her own body weight. She was in the living room looking out over the ocean, screaming and crying. I had no caregiver that day; sometimes they just didn't show up. It was on me to get Kat to drink, eat, and do catheters.

She was in deep despair, shaking her head back and forth, screaming, "No, no, no."

She had refused water, food, and catheters for a whole day, and I was getting desperate. I called Matt again. I needed help.

I also called Kat's doctor at the VA, which turned out to be a big mistake. I just opened the gates to hell and a world not equipped to handle these things. A world where everyone just protects themselves, not the patient. A world filled with contradictions. An Orwellian world where you literally go mad.

The doctor at the VA said they had to call the police if Kat wasn't drinking or eating, because she was a danger to herself. I knew that if they called the police, she would die. A person who has been abused and raped, multiple times, now paralyzed and manhandled by the police? She would not be able to take that. I immediately realized I was doomed. The doctors at the VA wanted to call the police. I wanted to call the ambulance, and Kat was inside screaming from the bottom of her lungs.

Matt came over with his wife, Cherrie. He tried everything, but to no avail. Kat was lost in the abyss.

I threatened to call the ambulance if Kat didn't drink, and I actually did call 911.

"911, how can I help?" And finally we heard something from Kat. She whispered, "Okay, okay," and the immediate danger was over.

I was emotionally done. I was still on epilepsy drugs, in a neck brace, physically weak, and now I was also totally emotionally drained.

This is where I gave up, even if just for a brief second.

I sat down under a tree on the top of our hill. I broke down and cried. I wanted out. I wanted to go away. I couldn't do this anymore. I did not want to do this anymore.

At the time, I didn't have the tools to cope, but I later set out on a journey to get the tools by listening to the entire library of Dr. Jordan Peterson, and later, his words have saved me more than once.

I called the VA again. "She is drinking and eating now," I said.

I was lying, and they were suspicious. It took all I had to get them off my back, and I would never turn to them for help again. I had to call them every three to four hours that day and for the next week to say Kat was back to her normal self, just to keep them off my back.

I have no contact with them now.

They failed me when I needed them the most.

I will never call them again.

Ever.

Kat's comment: "I screamed at you to not call 911. I hated you for wanting to take me to the VA or call 911. I hated that no one could understand my pain. You all were well. I had no desire for life."

CHAPTER 77

STRENGTH

AT MY LOWEST, I WANTED OUT, BUT I FOUND STRENGTH.

My best friend, Pauline, asked me where my strength comes from, and my go-to answer is that I love Kat, but even more so I love what Kat did for me before the accident. She made me adventurous and she made me a better man. I think in the best of relationships, you make each other stronger, you learn from each other, and you empower each other. You don't want your equal; you want your opposite. You want to learn from each other.

I stay true to myself and live day by day now, so I don't want to dwell in the past. I don't believe it will do me any good, and foremost, I believe it will deprive me of my present. You already know how I stood up to my stepdad when I was younger, so there was a sense of justice and action in me at an early age.

One more incident that stands out to me, where I took a stand for myself, was when I was drafted to do military service in Sweden. It was mandatory at the time, and not doing it was punished with a jail sentence.

CHAPTER 78

JAIL OR RANGER

What saved me from jail was a captain in the Swedish Air Force named Kenth Rubin.

I was a drifter until my late teens. I had all this energy, but I didn't know what to do with it. Looking back, I think it could have gone both ways. I could have become either a criminal or a highly productive member of society.

I was eighteen years old, and I had my mind set on becoming a coastal ranger; it's the elite of what the Swedish military has to offer.

I stood in front of Captain Kenth Rubin, and he said, "They tell me you want to go to jail."

I said, "Yes, if I can't be a ranger, I want to go to jail."

Refusing military service came with a mandatory jail sentence in Sweden at the time.

"Unfortunately, your asthma is preventing you from becoming a ranger, but is there anything else you are interested in?"

I looked at the captain and said, "Photography."

The captain looked at me and said, "Great, you will be working in our photography department helping develop film from our fighter jets, and taking photos of recruits and such. Report to that department immediately."

Captain Kenth and I later became friends, and he offered me a job at the Air Force Base after my year-long service was over. I respectfully declined. He had steered me onto a path I loved, and now there was no stopping me. I think he understood, and I hope he knew what he did for me. He changed the course of my life.

A lesser person would have sent me to jail, and what would have happened then? Would I have channeled all my energy into learning criminal skills? Yes, I think so.

I truly believe the environment we are in shapes us. There is always free will, but the environment determines the choices available to us.

Thank you, Captain Kenth Rubin. I hope you are proud of me. I am sure as hell proud of you.

CHAPTER 79

THE ABYSS

THE ABYSS WAS STILL CALLING MY NAME. I WAS DOWN AND out and had no way out. Little did I know that hope and help was literally just around the corner. The tide was shifting.

CHAPTER 80

CHAI

I KNOW EXACTLY WHEN I TOLD MYSELF, "WE ARE GOING TO be okay," and it was thanks to a Native American woman. Chai is a literal powerhouse, a strongman, and a CrossFit trainer. She owned a box, a CrossFit gym in Torrance near our Fighterdiet office.

I peeked into the garage gym, and two paralyzed women sat there working, one on the floor and one in her wheelchair. I walked in and was greeted with a big smile from Chai.

I said, "I'm just out walking on my lunch break and saw this gym."

I told my story about Kat, and Chai listened. Almost immediately, she said, "Let's do a fundraiser."

I didn't know if she was joking or just excited, but I thanked her. We said we'd be in touch.

Chai was a woman of her word. She put her troops in action, and no more than three months after, we had our first, big fundraiser at Brazil Strength. I was nervous. Would anyone show up? We had prepared CrossFit heats, food, a DJ, and local vendors. It was a big setup. One by one, they trickled in. It was as if they had come out of the woodwork, invisible at first, but then we saw groups of people, and those groups became a crowd. The crowd became hundreds. People were excited about the day and excited to meet Kat.

Colonel Wasson—remember him, the proud military man crying and asking Kat to do one more run? Well, he flew in from Colorado. People came from Belize, Air Force personnel in full force, all our nurses, all our friends. They all showed up!

I remember standing in the middle of the crowd, thinking, *We are going to be okay.*

I had a big smile on my face as I walked over and hugged Chai. She did more for us than she will ever know. She put my faith back in people. I knew we had tremendous support now, and my faith in humanity was restored. **True love.**

Our situation, and Kat herself, brings out the best in people. If you are ready to be a hero, to yourself and us, here was the chance. Chai was added to our list of heroes, and I mark this day as the day I knew we would make it. From here on, I started to rebuild our lives.

I also added my new mantra for life, *Hoka Hey*, a Native American saying loosely translated to "live so well that when your time comes, you die with a smile."

Patrizia, me, and Chai.

CHAPTER 81

WE HAVE TO MOVE

After the nurse drove our van into a wall, we knew we needed to move. We needed a flat house. We needed something relatively cheap, and we needed it now. It was a welcome distraction to go house hunting. Kat did all the work online and found a house in Hawthorne. It's located right outside the beach cities area in Los Angeles, home to Elon Musk's SpaceX. It's right at the cusp of a pretty rough area. Everyone warned us about buying in Hawthorne, because the city's reputation was not good.

The house was cute. Built in the 1950s with an adorable backyard. Rick, our realtor, was smart. He knew we could make this house into our own if we were lucky enough to get it. This is Los Angeles; competition was fierce even though it was located on the wrong side of town. There must have been fifty couples and singles looking at the house when I was there. At $700,000, it was in that "affordable range" for a couple or a well-off single. I saw some house flippers there too. The house could easily be flipped and sold for more.

We wrote a letter to the house owners, and they thankfully took Kat to heart and we got the house. It was a small house with small rooms and quite the opposite of what we needed, but we knew that. Matt, our angel, also a contractor, could help us. The plan was to gut the whole house down to the studs and basically make two big rooms with doors wide enough for Kat's wheelchair to fit through.

Demolition was scheduled for two weekends, and we had ordered a dump truck as big as the house to basically fit all of the insides into the dump truck. To save money, we told our friends to come help us demo the place, but we were unsure if anyone would show up.

Chris was one of the first ones, then Eddie Monge, then Air Force personnel, and then the NextStep trainers. We didn't need to worry. Everyone came, and we filled those dumpsters in no time. It was heartwarming to see the support.

In time, we built our little fifties house into a beautiful staycation oasis where Kat could feel peace. We received a VA grant to modify the house and make it accessible. All contractors, landscapers, concrete guys, and others gave huge discounts. Some did it at cost, but between the house purchase and the cost for the rebuild, we were strapped for cash.

Kat made our house into a staycation home resembling Belize. This helps her, since she spends so much time in bed and at home. I created an office upstairs, and I have my gym in the garage so I can be close to Kat at all times.

CHAPTER 82

YEAR ONE RECAP

Not the broken neck. Not the halo. Not the stroke I had after they took off the halo, which made me lose my ability to speak and write and pass out on the street. Not the opioids, not the epilepsy meds, not the years it took to rebuild myself physically.

All that was easy compared to seeing all my wife's dreams being taken away.

Kat doesn't let me see her pain. She keeps it together for me. I don't let her see my pain. I keep it together for her. But we know. Sometimes Kat cries and screams from the depth of her being. Those moments are terrifying. The pain I feel is indescribable.

There is no going back for us, for any of us. Death will be liberating. We don't want it, but we will embrace it when it's time. Our hearts won't be able to endure pain like this for a lifetime. We do not wish for eternal life. I shouldn't speak for Kat, but I know. No one can endure this forever.

We found **true love** in the twisted wreck of metal that was once a Range Rover. We found **true love** when we both decided to live, to fight, for ourselves and for each other. Neither one of us left or gave up. Neither of us took the easy way out.

She says she looks at me sometimes, wondering why I stay.

I stay with Kat because I have nowhere to run. I stay with Kat because it is the right thing to do.

I stay with Kat because I love her. God knows I wanted to run. I wanted to take my savings and run far far away, but I can never outrun myself. Wherever I go, I have to answer to myself.

I am no saint. I have many faults, but I respect myself. I will never leave Kat.

To be able to give fully is to first love oneself. We are born alone, and we will die alone. But if you can make peace with yourself, and know yourself, and be honest with yourself, nothing can hurt you, not even death.

CHAPTER 83

GOD, GRACE, OR WHAT?

I DID A LOT OF THINGS INTUITIVELY RIGHT THE FIRST YEAR. Actions and thought patterns just came to me. They say our greatest instinct is survival, and I am living proof of it.

Early on, I realized I had to fill my days with so much happiness that even though all these bad things happened, at least I started the day with a full happiness tank.

The strategy was simple. I would focus on my mental outlook, physical activities, and surround myself with encouraging people. I would try to live in a world full of endorphins, serotonin, and adrenaline—the body's own happiness drugs. Since the accident, I have become a physical powerhouse. My body is at this point a reflection of my mind. Strong mind, strong body.

By far, the biggest help I had and still have is to write. My first Facebook post after the accident was this:

I will come back FUCKING STRONGER than ever!

I will come back stronger for ME, for KAT and because there is no other way.

We not only conquer, we surpass previous accomplishments and DEMOLISH THEM with new ONES!

Watch us become STRONG again, watch us CONQUER!

WE HAVE LIFE & we will be adventurous.

Granted. I wasn't very eloquent in the beginning, but I was always honest and raw. It soon attracted a following and lifelong friendships.

"You taught me the gentle spirit & iron discipline. You inspire, teach and touch with your love and commitment to your beautiful wife."

—SHEVAUN WILLIAMS

CHAPTER 84

YEAR TWO, PEANUT SHOWS UP

One day Ashley, one of our caregivers, brought Peanut. He was a small Yorkie male, and Kat and I fell immediately in love. I never had a dog growing up as I am allergic and something childlike woke up in me when I could cuddle, play, and walk this hypoallergenic dog.

It wasn't long before Ashley left Peanut a day, two days, and even a week with us. Peanut would come up to me and tap me with his paws when he wanted to go out, and I loved walking him. Peanut would crawl up to Kat's face and lick her tears when she cried, and Peanut slept with us in our bed.

Peanut gave me the gift of accountability. He needed his walks, and he paid us back with licks to the face. It was pure love and such a bright spot in the daily grind.

I dreamingly asked Kat to get me a dog, and not long after, Kat got me Chapo—a puppy Yorkie named after the cartel leader, for his short legs and stocky appearance.

At the end of this story, we have four Yorkies, all filled with love and accountability: Chapo, Chico, Chula, and Mila, short for Milagro (the miracle).

CHAPTER 85

KAT'S BODY DETERIORATES

HER BODY FALLS APART SO FAST. IT SEEMED LIKE JUST EVERY week something new was happening with Kat, and she was forced to see herself disintegrate. Muscles atrophy really fast when they are not used, and when you are paralyzed, you can't use them at all. When muscles disappear, the body becomes unstable and boney. It was heartbreaking to see this former, strong, proud athlete see herself become a shadow of her former self. Her thick strong muscles were now loose skin over brittle bones. I never mention it. We both know. There's no need to talk about it.

Once athletic, muscular, and curvy, now skin and brittle bones.
Peanut, Kat, and me in bed.

"It must be a silent hell to feel Kat fade away. To know that you have done and still do and keep on doing all the best for her. It takes an emotional and concrete cost more than what can be expected. Shows that your character has given you strength. U have chosen to help instead of fleeing or just dying. Respect and admiration all the way. I know, just words. The hug is for real."

—DAD

CHAPTER 86

DEATH COMES CALLING

She whispered, "Costco."

Kat had been sitting outside a café in the sun talking to her friends, Carol and Jessica, when her body overheated. Kat started to feel disoriented.

I said, "Let's take her to the VA."

Kat whispered, "Costco freezer."

Cynthia and I understood what she meant. We knew by now what to do. We needed to cool Kat down, fast. An emergency room is no use. It takes more time explaining what to do, and they are not used to quadriplegics. Cynthia started driving. Fast! We drove through red lights as safely as we could. This was a true emergency. Kat's blood pressure and temperature can go up or down fast with little to no warning. The next step is a stroke, and that can lead to brain damage or death if untreated for too long.

We slammed open the doors and ran into Costco with Kat in front of us. We ran into the middle of the big walk-in vegetable refrigerator. We put frozen bags of food on Kat and poured ice cold water on her face. Kat was burning up! I knew death was close this time. Her voice was gone. Her eyes were locked in the distance. There was no response when talking to her.

We just stood there shivering from the cold while other shoppers strolled around us. Surreal. A Costco employee got upset. We had spilled water on the floor. He said it was slippery and people could fall. We tried to explain the emergency, but he didn't care. At least he left us alone. We stayed there until Kat became conscious again.

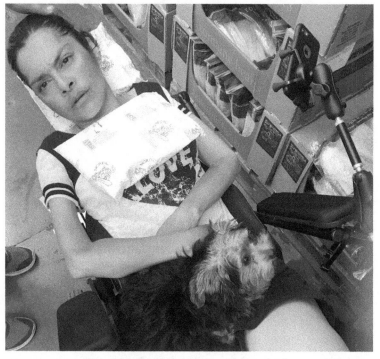

Kat in the walk-in fridge at Costco. Chapo on her lap.

These episodes became more frequent, and we now always have a bag packed in our car with the essentials—catheters, meds, blood pressure cup, etc.

CHAPTER 87

HOW LONG WILL
I LAST?

THE FIRST YEARS AFTER THE ACCIDENT, FIGHTERDIET STILL
had a regular office. I tried to stay at home as much as possible,
but I had to show my face a couple of days a week in the office.
Driving home from the office was knowing that once I came home,
my "second shift started." I was never off. It was either work in the
office or work with Kat.

The first year I was just waiting for the doctor to tell me "you
have cancer, and it's stress-related."

The first year, I was in a constant fight-or-flight mode. Always on
the edge. I remember coming home from work one day, exhausted,
and I started crying when one of the nurses had washed the dishes
for me. That's how tired I was.

Ironically, that is what I had asked my mom to come and do
for us. "Please come over, even just for a month and help out with
simple stuff like the dishes."

But she never came.

There are no off-days when you are paralyzed or caring for
someone who is paralyzed.

CHAPTER 88

A BETTER MAN

It took many years before I saw it as a privilege to help Kat and not as work. That mental shift made all the difference in the world. All of a sudden, I tapped into my superpowers and had another level of mental and physical strength. It is all about purpose. With the right purpose, your mind and body will always be there for you.

"He who has a Why to live for can bear almost any How."

–NIETZSCHE

I wish I could say I had an "aha moment," but I didn't. It was the accumulative work I did on myself over the years after the accident. The combined wisdom of thousands of years before me distilled down into podcasts I listened and learned from. What truly separated me from many is that I put that wisdom in action and that slowly changed me into a better man.

"Give and you shall receive." I get goosebumps writing it even though I am not a believer. It is truly so. When I started giving without expecting anything in return, it came back to me exponentially.

Mentally, when I saw it as an honor to help Kat every day, my inner reward system exploded every day and gave me strength, self-respect, and superpowers.

CHAPTER 89

BEGGING FOR MONEY

We knew we were living on borrowed time, and we knew Kat would lose her 24/7 care when the Air Force medically discharged her. We knew we both had to be productive and solve the coming caregiver and money crisis.

By the end of year two, I had sold everything I owned, and I had emptied out my dad's nest egg. Terje had been more than giving, and his money gave us breathing room.

Some say they can never ask for money. But when you are faced with the prospect of personal bankruptcy and committing your wife to a nursing home, well, then you do what you have to do to keep your wife's dignity.

We established a "nurse account." There was a substantial amount in there at one point, but it was quickly drained as every month we had to pull out over $10,000 for caregivers.

It was a battle destined to be lost. We would keep our heads above water, for a while. But who can keep that up? Ten thousand dollars a month just for caregivers. To that, you have to add mortgage, food, car insurance, etc.

CHAPTER 90

NICOLE IS A BELIEVER AND A DOER

We are on our own now. Kat's insurance has run out.

One day she was just here—a real life angel with a protein jar full of one dollar bills. Nicole was a believer and she was a doer. Her contributions made a real difference. Nicole had an infectious smile. In spite of having real hardships in her life, she found a way to help us. She worked as a waitress and took all her tips and saved them in a huge protein jar. When the jar was full, she either sent it to us, or she came and visited. I was and am full of respect for Nicole. She was struggling hard herself but found a way to still give to us.

Kat and I made it, thanks to Nicole and many like her. It took us years to find a sustainable way to cover the cost of caregivers, and while we were fighting, people gave us hundreds of thousands of dollars. I can't name you all, but you know who you are, and you made a difference.

How we paid caregivers the first two years, in dollar bills.
Real bills from real payouts made to nurses.

A real life angel, Nicole.

CHAPTER 91

I REACHED OUT TO NICOLE BEFORE THE RELEASE OF THE BOOK

I first was introduced to you in Fighterdiet.

I was a caregiver for my mother in law for four years. It was pretty much 24/7, except working four nights at the restaurant. When I heard about the accident, I was asked to pray for you both because we did not know details just yet. I began saving all my single dollars from my tips.

So I prayed. I prayed for wisdom. What could a young woman do whose marriage was abusive and had lost hope in life? When later I discovered you needed help, I remembered how few people helped me when I escaped my own house. I saw the jar I had with dollar bills and started saving every single $1.

I had so much hidden debt after leaving my marriage, but I needed faith, if I helped someone else in their time of need, God might help me. I knew the sacrifice it takes to care for a loved one 24/7, so the journey began. My heart ached to have my mother-in-law still here. Her being alive made the marriage bearable, but it was not living.

Your love and dedication for your wife gave me hope to live myself, so I did whatever I could, even used Venmo once, when I couldn't travel.

−Nicole

CHAPTER 92

STOP BEING A LITTLE BITCH, PAVEL

IF I EVER FEEL LOW OR FEEL SORRY FOR MYSELF, I LOOK AT Kat working with her stick and I stop feeling like a baby and get back to it. Kat fought herself off the ventilator, back to breathing on her own, and that determination showed itself when it came time to communicate and work too.

Kat likes to stay busy. Together with Matt, they jerry-rigged one of the IV poles at the VA to allow Kat to lie in bed, on her side, and communicate and read and do all the things you and I normally do. To this day, we still have that IV pole, and we still use that setup for her iPhone. When Kat sits up in bed, we have a small plastic table that we use as a base for her iPad Pro.

Kat works on her iPad with the help of a stick (stylus). She points, swipes, and clicks with it. Siri is used for texting using her voice or to call people. She does more with her "one finger" than most do with ten.

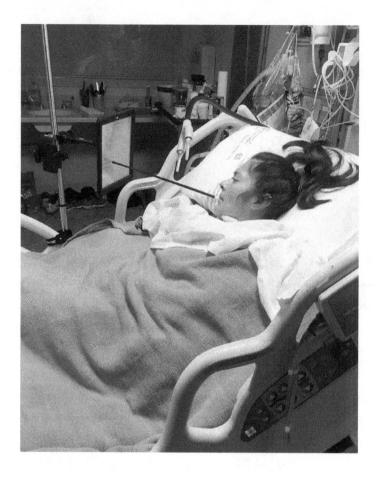

What does it do to a man when the first thing he hears is: "I want to die."

Year two was foggy for me. We were alive, but I am not sure we were living. I researched how to die. Where is it legal? Was suicide an option? How? The ever-present sadness and talk about death and pain—I think it is like war. It must be. It slowly erodes your soul.

I laid with Kat in bed, held her in my arms while she cried and screamed herself to sleep. Her screams came from deep down, from the core of her being. Despair, anxiety, and death. We talked about options for legal suicide many many times, and the subject still comes up from time to time.

Before the accident, I didn't love Kat the way I should have. I found out later she did not love me the way she should have. There were many times we should have been loving but were not. A horrible accident made us open our eyes, and we would both kill to start over again, this time with our eyes open. But that will never happen. Kat is paralyzed from her neck down, she cannot move her arms or legs, and she has trouble breathing. She needs twenty-four/seven nurse care. That is our life now and probably for the rest of our lives.

Neither Kat nor I saw a bright light. We saw only darkness and pain. I yelled and cried and said "fuck you" to both the Devil and God, but neither showed their face. I let my anger out on priests for a while, provoking them with questions like, "Where is God now?" And "Why is this happening?" But I stopped and the priests stopped coming to visit too.

What filled the void was love. **True love for each other and true love for our heroes.**

CHAPTER 93

I HAVE PTSD

It's like a ghost living in your brain, fucking with you. I am an addict because of it. I have to shut the demon up, and I do. I use the gym for my endorphin kick. I beat myself up hard, every day.

Whiskey makes me go to sleep. I don't drink during the day. I only drink to relax in the evening and to shut up the demons that taunt me. To stop the brain from spinning. To get saved by sleep, at least for five to six hours.

I hate Facebook Memories. I can't look at photos pre-accident. I just can't. They remind me of the life we were supposed to have. I want to go back. I want to go back to everyday problems, watching *Housewives of Orange County*, complaining about my latte at Starbucks, and my white picket fence life.

We never asked to inspire anyone. We want to go back in time and be an ordinary, average Joe.

We want nothing to do with being inspirational because it hurts. Inspiration is born out of pain—unimaginable physical and mental pain.

We have no choice. We are strong because we have to be.

I fuel myself and work out in order to have energy for the next thirty to forty years, but I know when it's all over, it will be a welcome rest for me. I have no illusions about death. I have no fear, and I have no hopes or wants of an afterlife.

Hoka Hey. Do you remember what it meant?

"To live so well that when your time comes you can die with a smile."

CHAPTER 94

AIR FORCE "LEAVE NO MAN BEHIND"

ALTHOUGH YEAR TWO WAS ROUGH, IT HAD A FEW BRIGHT lights. One was a birthday party I arranged for Kat. She had her suspicions when I blindfolded her and we drove around the block in circles to disorient her. We came to a stop at a local place called Pancho's, and inside were forty to fifty of her closest friends waiting, including many from the Air Force.

I stood across the table from the general. I was thanking him and all of Kat's Air Force friends for being there for Kat and me, from the day of the accident until now. I had seen "leave no man behind" in action or, as they say, in the Air Force, "your wingman." I had experienced it, and it is the most beautiful thing in the world. It's real. I was crying when I gave my speech, but I wasn't ashamed of my tears. They were tears of joy and thankfulness. All of us there that day had played a part in us surviving.

We got a little wild in the restaurant. A piñata was hanging from the second floor, and we took turns hammering it with a bat. One of Kat's Air Force colleagues, Annie, even showed off her Tae Kwon Do skills and roundhouse-kicked the poor piñata. The birthday became the highlight of the year, and soon thereafter

Kat's retirement ceremony made the year feel even a little bit better. The comradery between military service members is untouchable.

Kat's retirement ceremony was held in our backyard. More than fifty Armed Forces members attended our small celebration, and even the general and vice commander of Los Angeles Air Force base attended. I was so nervous, I poured whiskey into a coffee cup. As I stood and watched the ceremony, I slowly sipped it. I was awarded a certificate for being Kat's spouse at the ceremony. It wasn't so much the plaque; it was the servicemen gathered, looking at me as I approached Kat, kissed her on the cheek, and nodded thank you. I never became a Swedish Special Forces ranger, but I gained the respect of all these US Air Force service members and that mattered to me. It mattered a lot.

Still, almost five years after the accident, generals, airmen, contractors—they all check in, come visit, call, email, and stay true to their "fallen comrade."

Kat and her commander, Brigadier General Philip Garrant.

CHAPTER 95

TRAUMA SURVIVOR MEETING

ONE DAY, A LETTER ARRIVED INVITING US BACK TO WHERE IT all started—Long Beach Memorial Hospital.

It was a trauma survivor meeting, and they really wanted us there. Kat and I were both a bit anxious to go back there, but we did.

Kat sat by a table while I was getting refreshments. I saw our neurosurgeon, Dr. Nargess, and smiled.

I approached her and she leaned in toward me and said, "I thought she would have taken her life by now."

I looked at Dr. Nargess and realized right then and there that no one really believed we would make it. Not friends, not family, not even the doctors. And I fall. I fall into the abyss.

I fall only to be lifted up by the same person, minutes later.

We are all sitting down around a table, and Dr. Nargess looks at me, takes my hands in hers, and shakes them vigorously, saying, "You are a real man. You are a real man."

I kept shaking her hands, looking at her while she repeated the words.

Finally, Kat had to tell me to let go of the doctor's hands. I held her hands so long because when you respect someone that much and they look at you with admiration, you don't want to let go.

Dr. Nargess was always brutally honest. Proving her wrong, that Kat was alive and thriving, was only a tribute to her own work.

We proved a lot of people wrong the first two years after the accident.

CHAPTER 96

YEAR THREE

We are finding our "new normal" this year. We are still fumbling around trying to make sense of it all, trying to accept our new reality, but we are trying to live a little bit more, and we are finding new routines.

There is a show called *Al Extremo* on cable. I don't even understand how it is allowed to air, but it's Mexican and it shows the most horrific, brutal videos I have ever seen. Men cut in half by cars with their guts hanging out, pleading for help. People with their limbs chopped off by Mexican cartels, many still alive. This is all mixed with a video collage of that day's "hottie," a sexy, curvy, lightly dressed pinup model showing tits and ass and then boom! Back to gore, guts, machetes, and screams.

Kat used to watch this endlessly at night, and I get it. It made her feel better that there were people out there actually worse off than her. When you are paralyzed from the neck down, there are not a lot of people worse off than you, but these people were. She was also intrigued by prisoners and prison shows. She compared her life to them. After all, they had both lost their freedom in some way.

It's just human nature, and whatever helps, helps. So we sat there in the evenings watching people suffer, die, and be killed. I watched it with her, but couldn't see it all. I had to look away or close my eyes when it became too gruesome. That is how we got through a lot of evenings this year.

Eventually we stopped watching, but the show is still on.

CHAPTER 97

IT'S LIKE YOU ALMOST DON'T HAVE TO CARE TO SURVIVE

My ex-wife Pauline said, "It's like you almost don't have to care just to get by," and she was right. If you live in the darkness 24/7, you will perish.

I take a trip every three months or so just to get away. It is one of my steam valves, but it's also my way of feeling normal. It's almost like I am another person when I travel. Not that I lie about who I am, but for a short period of time, I do allow myself just to care about myself and live with absolutely no responsibilities. I often end up in Belize, and I do the same thing every trip. Paddleboard, eat grilled fish caught the same day at the restaurant El Fogon, work out. All alone and very happy.

When I had truly awakened and discovered my new self, these trips became more about giving back and helping others in need, on the poorer parts of the island.

CHAPTER 98

DREAMS

I DREAMT KAT WOKE UP AND SHE COULD MOVE HER ARMS. I yelled at her, "Careful, careful. Don't overdo it." I was afraid her brittle bones would break. She continued moving her arms and she had the biggest smile on her face. Then I woke up.

We are condemned to this life now. There is no hope for Kat to regain mobility. No real hope. There is always a wish, a dream, but in real everyday life, it is not something we talk about anymore. It is about survival now. Our lives are so fragile. We both work so diligently to create routines and stick to them to get through the day, but then a caregiver quits, and our world is thrown into chaos. Recently a caregiver had to leave due to respiratory issues, and we were without a caregiver four nights a week.

Being a caregiver at night is a tough job. A tough job we ask people to do for minimum wage as that is what we can afford. Kat's mom saved us this time. She flew in from Chicago and was a night caregiver for two weeks. **True love.**

Hope for mobility would return, year four.

CHAPTER 99

CAREGIVERS

I HAVE STOPPED COUNTING HOW MANY CAREGIVERS WE HAVE gone through, but it's literally hundreds.

I have stopped counting the number of arguments Kat and I had. I sometimes felt I was never enough for Kat. I was never enough for myself. I was never enough for my company. It was a totally unwinnable situation, and at times, I was just waiting to break down. Sometimes I wanted myself to break down to have a way out of this. But I always found extra energy and extra will to continue. I found much of that energy through my writing. Sharing my story with you on Facebook and hearing your stories, your responses, your feedback.

Kat's comment:

Thank you, babe. I sometimes think it's best I was the one paralyzed and not you. Mainly because of the VA. Imagine. Your insurance cut you off after $100k. What if you were the one paralyzed? How would we make it financially? How would you deal with paralysis? It would be challenging for me to be at work and make sure you had care. It would be challenging for me to transfer you. We would be in a small apartment. Oftentimes I wonder if paralysis is better than my death. What would life be like if I did completely break my neck and died? I thank you for your care, sacrifices, and unrelenting love. ♥ ♥ Paralysis is extreme but it's best I'm the one paralyzed and not you.

CHAPTER 100

BEGGING FOR CARE

MANY PARALYZED PEOPLE KILL THEMSELVES DUE TO IGNO-rance and unbearable pain. Being forced to get care from other people, people you may not like, and people who may abuse you verbally, physically, or simply just by being ignorant.

The worst are the ones saying, "Try to be happy," or "I under-stand you," or the ones who tell Kat "to move," or the ones who don't listen to Kat and do what they want to do, not what Kat wants them to do. Or the ones who say, "You just have to turn your life over to God," not knowing Kat was a believer before the accident and now she is not because of the accident. I watch from the side-lines. I step in when I have to but I try not to.

There were different reasons and justifications that priests, pas-tors, and other believers came up with as to why God allowed the accident. Some said it was karma from what her ancestors had done. Some said God let the accident happen for a reason. Some said that this is Kat's cross to bear so other people can be inspired. All these excuses to justify God's actions left Kat confused. The truth is, no one knows, of course, and if you ask Kat today, she believes in people's love, family, and friends' love.

I believe it is random. There is no meaning or higher purpose with our accident, but what came out of it was a lot of love and grace, selflessness, and heroism. People being their best self to help Kat. That in itself was "godlike" to witness.

I have lost my temper more than once. I get so angry when Kat is mistreated. I get angry at myself too for not being able to provide better care. We are asking minimum wage people to provide the best care. We are asking minimum wage people to be as organized and efficient as me and Kat. We can't afford to pay more, so we have to lower our expectations. More than once, Kat and I become inspirateurs and educators for our nurses. They see what we have achieved in life, and they get inspired by it. We are happy to help and it has created lifelong friendships. But it has also created frustration, anger, and suicidal thoughts.

CHAPTER 101

FORGET PRIDE— THIS IS SURVIVAL

Year three was better. Our routines were settling in, but it was not without their challenges.

She was crying. I was on my knees and I was begging her to stay.

I had been working out in the garage when the caregiver walked past me.

I asked, "Where are you going?"

She said, "Home."

I said, "But your shift isn't over yet."

She responded, "My son needs me."

I lost it. I yelled at her. "You are at your job, taking care of a paralyzed woman and you are just going to leave? What if I wasn't here, would you just leave her all alone?" I was furious.

She started crying. She wasn't even a caregiver, she was the mom to a caregiver we had. The caregiver had suggested that her mom could help out as we desperately needed more help. We liked her mom, she had taken us in for Thanksgiving and made us feel part of their family. She had made food especially for me. Kat loved their presence and being part of their holiday celebrations.

But this day I would ruin all that.

I totally lost it. I was tired and angry. We were all in the bedroom, all crying. I went down on my knees asking the mom to forgive me for yelling, and asking if she would stay and work for us. I swallowed all my pride but to no avail. We never saw the caregiver or her mom again. The mom didn't deserve to be yelled at. I destroyed years of friendship in one big outburst.

I felt worthless.

You see, desperation is always just beneath the surface. We are constantly trying to survive by raising money and hiring new caregivers. There is no off-day from being paralyzed.

CHAPTER 102

FINANCIAL RELIEF AT LAST

Janne Kouri, the founder of NextStep, invited us over to meet the CEO of The Wounded Warrior project. Janne wanted Kat there to work out to show the NextStep operations. Kat is always very charming and easy to talk to, and Kat took the opportunity and connected with the CEO.

Kat then worked with The Wounded Warrior Project for one year. Numerous emails and phone calls, till one day they decided to step in and offset much of the cost we had to privately fund for our caregivers. That day was such a victory! We could breathe again! I remember feeling such relief.

We cancelled the fundraisers we had planned for this year. We were so tired after fighting nonstop for three years, depleting our funds, depleting our friends' funds, depleting my dad's funds, that we just stopped. We allowed ourselves to sit back and just relax for a bit.

Later we would start giving back to others what others had given to us.

CHAPTER 103

SHAME ON YOU!

ROSA WAS HERE VISITING US AND HELPING OUT. OUR CARE-giver, Rosa, and Kat took the van down to the local shopping mall. Kat was in her electric wheelchair.

I got a FaceTime call from Kat. She looked sad. "Can you come and get me?" she asked.

I didn't ask why, I jumped on my bicycle and hurried down to the mall. Kat was sitting in her electric wheelchair in the corner of the store, in the "hall of shame" looking very sad.

The back of her wheelchair had grabbed onto a clothing rack by mistake and as Kat drove in between the racks, she had pulled down a whole row of clothing racks. The owner had gotten furious!

"What are you dooiing? Stooop! Stoooop the chaiiiiir."

Kat was embarrassed but we laughed so hard once we got out of the store. It was such a relief to laugh again. The laughter would start to come more often now.

CHAPTER 104

FORTUNE LADY AND HEALERS

ACCEPTING THE FACT THAT KAT WAS PARALYZED FROM THE neck down and making a new life based on those circumstances is what I had to do to survive. And what Kat had to do.

Unfortunately, there are misguided people everywhere. One of our caregivers preyed on Rosa and made her believe that Kat could be healed. She took Kat's mom to a fortune teller in downtown Los Angeles. Rosa paid $10,000 for Kat to be able to move again.

How did we find out? A Chicago detective called us. Rosa had called the police in Chicago after Kat didn't get better. We never saw that $10,000 again.

In a way, it is very sweet and heartbreaking to see what a mom would do to get her daughter back to before the accident, but it's also what I have been battling this whole time. That people do what they want to do to help, not what I need them to do. I needed caring hands to help me take care of Kat and chores at our house, but our families wanted to find "other people or other solutions" to not have to be there themselves. Many times, people refer to "God" and prayers instead of actually helping with their own hands.

I would have been better off using that $10,000 for better care-givers than to give it to an oracle in downtown Los Angeles.

My sister researched doctors to help us when all I needed was for her to come visit for an hour when she was here on vacation anyway. I had all the doctors in the world. I needed a familiar friendly face to make Kat happy, if only for an hour visit.

My mom said she was too old to help out when all I needed from her was to help do the dishes, something she does every day at home.

Why did our own families and many friends go to such lengths not to help us? You have to ask them.

CHAPTER 105

BELIEVERS

BELIEVERS CAN BE SO MISGUIDED. GROWN MEN AND WOMEN that say "Kat can be healed" by some healer that never seems to materialize but everyone talks about. In the hospital I prayed with them, willing to try anything. Later I argued with them. Now I just look them in the eyes and they always look away.

Be careful about acting like a healer around people with real injuries. The bluff is too easily called.

CHAPTER 106

YEAR FOUR, OUR EVERYDAY IS SO FRAGILE

PEOPLE ARE FAST TO JUDGE. THEY ALL WANT A SCAPEGOAT, someone to put their own misery on. Someone to blame. This time was no different. I was once again blamed, and this time it almost broke me. Not the blame, per se, but I was running out of energy to deal with all our misfortune.

Kat laid on her side working on her phone. I was in the living room on the couch, really just a few feet away. Kat had let the daytime caregiver go home early, so it was just her and I. When Kat is in the same position for a long time, she can get involuntary spasms. Her whole body tenses up and relaxes in a fast jerk-like motion, like a coiled spring under a lot of tension. This time Kat felt the spasm coming and she tried to hold it back but she couldn't. Her muscles contracted hard and released in a fast jerk-like motion and propelled her whole body into a forward movement.

I was in the living room and I heard "Nooooooooo," followed by an awful sounding thud! Something hit the ground, hard. I was only a few feet away but the distance from the living room to our bedroom was a thousand yards that day. I ran into the bedroom, saw the bed, and Kat was not in it. I was not prepared for what was to come.

On the stone floor, face down, was Kat, and there was blood everywhere. Kat had spasmed so hard she had fallen out of bed, catching the fall with her head on the metal IV pole. I carefully turned her and wiped handfuls of blood from her face to see where the wound was.

Terrified, I called 911, "Please come, my paralyzed wife fell out of her bed. Please come."

Kat, as usual cool under pressure, said, "Find the wound, apply pressure."

She was calm but also scared. She was crying and so was I, because I could not find the wound due to all the blood. Finally, I saw the crack by the bridge of the nose and pushed linen onto her face and started calling for help. I had this down by now. I called Matt, I called Pauline, I called Chris.

Within ten minutes, I had the fire truck and ambulance there to help me. They took over.

I yelled to Chris, "Find Kat's green bag in the van. Get it to me."

I grabbed my own rescue bag and followed Kat into the ambulance. Chris handed me the green bag, our traveling bag with extra catheters and diapers. I told Chris to take care of the house and Chapo, our Yorkie. Chris just nodded. Military men know what to do.

And off we went to the emergency room again. This was the fourth time. First the main accident, then I stroked out, then the nurse crashed the car into the wall, and now Kat falls out of bed.

Immediately at the hospital, they separated me from Kat. They wanted to talk to Kat privately, to make sure she was not abused. I was quickly let back in and actually put to work. They were short staffed, so I found an empty hospital bed, lifted Kat up and pulled out a catheter kit from the green bag.

Kat was eventually sewn up with seven stitches at the bridge of her nose and we got to return home after a long night in the emergency room.

A caregiver of ours heard of the incident and told people there is no way Kat could have fallen out of bed, indirectly blaming me because I was the only one at home with her.

I asked the caregiver, "Do you understand what you are suggesting? You are suggesting that I pushed Kat out of bed, since you claim she couldn't spasm and fall out of bed."

She was silent. She refused to take responsibility for her own statement but was more than willing to just throw out blame.

This was and still is a recurring theme for me: people's willingness to assert guilt without any information whatsoever. When confronted—and I do confront them—they all turn out to be cowards.

No one stands up for their words to my face.

Today we have video cameras. It is for security and safety reasons, for everyone, and Kat can pull up the cameras and see what is going on in other rooms and around the exterior.

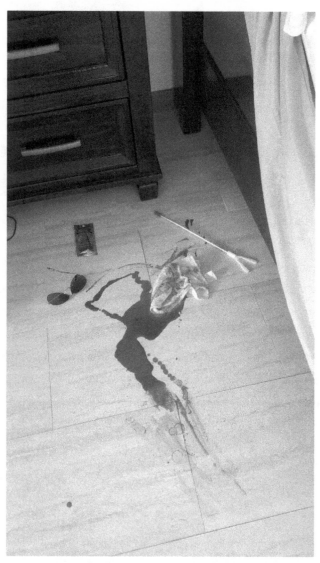

The aftermath of Kat falling out of bed.

CHAPTER 107

WHO TAKES CARE OF WHOM?

THE GREEN GRASS BEHIND THE WHITE FENCE WAS SLOWLY coming alive for me, not the way I had envisioned it, but in a different way.

The caregivers are Kat's hands and feet, and Kat makes sure they take care of me through their hands and feet. She makes sure there is food in the fridge; she finds recipes for the caregivers to cook for me. She buys me clothes online. She pays bills. She makes sure our house is in order.

We are a family now. Husband and wife and four Yorkies. We are what we both dreamed to have. Not in the way we expected it, but still a family who loves and takes care of each other. We created this little happy spot where we can take care of each other just like we both always dreamt of having security and warmth around us.

All of a sudden there was room to do more than "just survive." Both Kat and I lifted our eyes above the horizon and started setting new goals and started dreaming again.

Kat started taking online courses to get her second master's in psychology, and I was reinvigorated at work, in fitness, and in helping others. We had both healed enough to start to blossom again. We had gotten over "the three-year hump" that I read so much about. Perish or thrive. The three-year mark is where many give up.

It was incredibly liberating to have everyday problems again. Somehow Kat and I weren't afraid anymore. It was a measure of normality to be concerned about the lack of almond milk in the fridge instead of being afraid the day nurse would not show up. We had been through so much that we had settled into a day-by-day groove. We took it as it came. No nurse? No problem!

CHAPTER 108

ARE YOU A PERVERT?

Year four, we are finding our way. Our new way.

Even paralyzed from the neck down, Kat still had an appetite for life and for adventures! I was amazed that one day she said, "Let's go to Vegas!" and so we did. We packed ourselves into our van with our caregiver and off we went. We saw Jennifer Lopez in concert, we ate out, and we fell into bed, drunk, Vegas style, with the caregiver on the couch and me and Kat in bed.

It was good to be back in Vegas. It was the same hotel we had stayed in back when we first met and laid and snuggled on the couch.

On the way home, in the middle of the desert, Kat needed a catheter. We looked out the car windows for a place but it was just sand everywhere. It got more and more desperate as Kat could feel her blood pressure rising. Finally, a small town! We exited the highway and drove to the only motel there.

I jumped out of the car, rushed into the motel lobby, and said, "It's not what you think, but I need a room for half an hour," while waving cash around.

The hotel manager looked at me, sized me up, nodded, and said, "Right, buddy," with a wink. He said, "Forty bucks," and gave me the keys.

We all laughed. Who rents a room for half an hour? Only pimps and prostitutes—oh and quadriplegics who need a catheter done.

CHAPTER 109

ANGEL DE AMOR

ONE OF OUR BIGGER DONORS, MICKEY JACOBER, TALKED TO me about starting a nonprofit. She said, "It's easier for wealthy people to give to a nonprofit."

She was right; it is tax deductible and regulated. Just like everything else, fundraising is a business. If you want people to give, you have to present them with a reason why, and you are competing with many other fundraisers for the same money.

Kat has always been a giver. She taught me the pleasures and rewards of giving. Out of our misfortune, something beautiful blossomed: Kat's nonprofit foundation Angel De Amor, "Angel of Love."

Elsy Wity, Kat's childhood friend from Belize, had sent some photos over messenger. It was a man sitting on the ground, Elsy holding her arm around him. He was very dirty, and a catheter bag for his urine was visible strapped to his leg. Another photo showed a bag attached to his stomach where his bowel movement came out. It looked infected and his feet were swollen and filled with pus.

The man was Maynor. He was paralyzed from the waist down and lived on the streets making watercolor paintings and begging for a living. A store owner had come out and kicked his stuff over and asked him to get lost. That is how Elsy found him, crying, sitting on the ground with his few belongings scattered about.

Kat couldn't help herself. She went into full action, and it was such a pleasure to see.

Within a day, she had called upon her troops in Belize, and Maynor was on his way to be set up in a temporary shelter, a simple room with a shower and a toilet. It wasn't much, but it was safe from the streets. Kat arranged for Maynor to go to the local clinic and get his feet bandaged. The doctor wanted to amputate them, but Maynor refused.

Catheter bag.

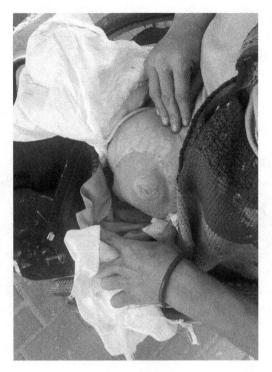

Colostomy bag.

Our caregivers borrowed medical supplies and gave them to Kat; friends came over with clothes; Mickey Jacober gave quite a lot of money. We set up a fundraiser for Maynor. Not long after, I went down to Belize with three suitcases full of medical supplies, clothes, and everyday things for his small room.

Maynor, in his new temporary home, surrounded by gifts we brought from Los Angeles.

Me, Maynor, and Elsy.

Both Kat and I were invigorated. We had a mission, we had purpose beyond just pure survival. Many on the island asked why we did it. The answer for us was simple. We saw a person in dire need, just like we had been. Helpless, we counted on people to help us. Now we could pay it forward and help someone in dire straits. **True love.**

When you have been as helpless as we were, and you see someone else with the same need, you literally feel their pain and they see that you understand them and the pain they are in. That connection alone is so deep and profound and full of meaning that it empowers you to do all you can to help.

Kat didn't even wait for our fundraiser to finish. She contracted a local builder and within a couple of months, we had built Maynor a real house. The first ADA-compliant house on the island, complete with shower, bedroom, and kitchen. We raised $10,000, and that is 20,000 BZE, which is enough to build a 16 × 16 one-level house, with a wheelchair ramp and all.

Painting the red door and the rest of the house white.
A bright beacon of light in the middle of all poverty.

Elsy Wity, our god-sent angel on the island, donated the land to build Maynor's house on. A renewed sense of me had emerged. I was not the same Pavel anymore. I was a better version of me now. Giving and empathetic.

Maynor outside his new home.

Elsy found more people on the island who needed help. Martha, like Maynor, was also paralyzed from the waist down. We got her a new wheelchair via the wheelchair foundation and arranged for food to be brought to her every week.

A little child named Giselle had hydranencephaly (part of her brain was filled with fluids). We shipped down boxes of formula and a blender so her mom could blend the food and feed her through a tube. These were happy times. We were both happy to be able to help.

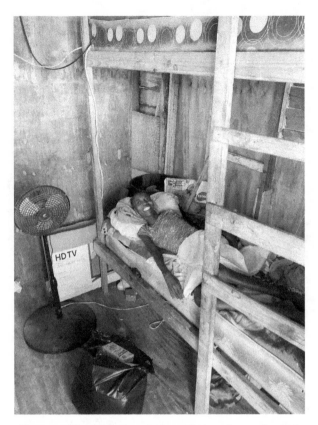

Martha, paralyzed from the waist down. Her home is a wooden shack.

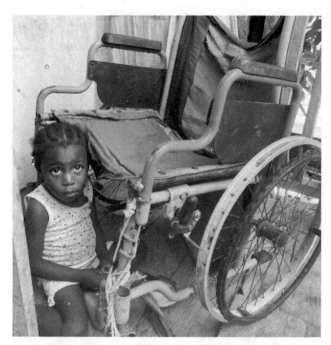

Martha's old wheelchair.

CHAPTER 110

TEAM HOYT

Kat sent me an article about Dick and Rick Hoyt. Rick has cerebral palsy and is confined to a wheelchair and can't control his limbs.

Excerpt from teamhoyt.com:

In the spring of 1977, Rick Hoyt told his father, Dick Hoyt, that he wanted to participate in a 5-mile benefit run for a lacrosse player who had been paralyzed in an accident. Far from being a long-distance runner, Dick agreed to push Rick in his wheelchair and they finished all 5 miles, coming in next to last. That night, Rick told his father, "Dad, when I'm running, it feels like I'm not disabled."

Dick and Rick are now legends, having completed numerous marathons and triathlons, and they even have their own team, Team Hoyt!

Kat after running Camp Pendleton with the Air Force track team.

CHAPTER 111

TANIA

I WAS MOVED BY THE ARTICLE. BEFORE THE ACCIDENT, KAT and I had run numerous races together, 5K, 10K, a mud run at Camp Pendleton, and even the big Rock 'n Roll race in San Diego the day after the mud run at Camp Pendleton. Here was an opportunity to run together again!

I contacted Team Hoyt. Tania Zamora at Team Hoyt–San Diego responded. Before we knew it, we had a specially built Team Hoyt wheelchair called a blade I could push Kat in, and we were signed up for a race. It was the same race we had run together just four years before, in San Diego.

This time, it was different though. We were both nervous. It wasn't so much about the running as it was saying to life itself, we are back! We are here and we are not giving up.

The Rock 'n Roll organizers let the blade start first, and Tania told me, "Stay to the right to let the other runners pass."

Boom! We were off and I had no intention of letting anyone pass. I ran full out from the start. I managed to keep the regular runners behind me for quite a while, and the bystanders were cheering us on.

Kat said, "Slow down, pace yourself," but I was racing for life, I was racing from death, and I was not slowing down.

Across the finish line, I couldn't speak. I just kneeled down next to Kat and sat there. We both proved that we wanted to live that day. We proved to ourselves that we were back and we were going to keep on accomplishing great things!

As I write this, the pandemic is raging in America and the world. I have continued to run and I am up to half marathons and practicing for my first Olympic-length triathlon. As soon as COVID subsides, I will be back with Team Hoyt. I don't think Kat will race with me anymore.

The pain of not being able to run is too much for her, but she did say, "You were not ashamed of me."

No, I was not ashamed of my wife being in a Team Hoyt blade. I was the proudest I have ever been. We both conquered our demons that day.

This was something we both needed to do. Somehow, it was resetting our way of life.
We showed ourselves we could still run, but we never ran a race together again.

CHAPTER 112

IT TOOK ME FOUR YEARS TO LOOK BACK WITHOUT CRYING

Swipe left, and I have no worries in the world. Swipe right, and I am in hell on earth. My last picture on my camera roll before the accident and my first one after the accident. I swipe back and forth, back and forth, back and forth. It makes no sense to do it, but I do it.

It's the same with Facebook memories. Those milestone moments Facebook picks for you and chooses to display on the top of your feed. I hated those. I scrolled past them as fast as I could. This year, Facebook started showing memories after the accident instead of before as enough time had passed. I look at them now, cautiously. It's like that first dip in the ocean. You can't just dive in. You have to dip your toe into the water and get your whole body used to what is to come. If you go too fast, you will shock your body and it will be too much. You can drown. Same with Facebook memories. I look at it sort of from an angle, scroll past it, and sometimes I go back and click on the image.

CHAPTER 113

ROSA

We have fought with each other from day one in the hospital. Rosa wanted God to help Kat, but God never came. I wanted Rosa to stay in Los Angeles to help me take care of Kat, but Rosa went back to Chicago.

In the hospital, I screamed, "Who do you think is going to wipe Kat's ass—God?"

Rosa tried to sue me. She thought I had crashed the car to collect insurance money. It is all so absurd to even write this, but in her eyes, someone had to take the blame and that someone was me.

It took me four years to really listen to Rosa and her own story. She finally said a few words that made me reevaluate everything, and now I understand and love her. I took the time to understand her. Off and on during those four and a half years after the accident, Rosa would come and visit. It was always tense, and I always felt the blame in her eyes. I played nice, for Kat's sake.

During her last visit, things changed. We got into a huge fight. I finally took the time to listen to her. In broken English, she told me her story while wiping her tears. She had been forced to work at three years old. Raped. No vacation, ever. Her story about child labor, rape, and unbelievable hardship in Honduras was then relived by her own daughter. Same story, different place, with Kat.

She would beat Kat to a pulp, and at one time, almost to death. I understand how desperate Rosa was. Always with different men, trying to find one to care for her. Rosa was just trying to survive.

We understood each other now. I understood why she couldn't help me right after the accident. She had to keep going, work, work, work. It is all she knew, to keep going, to survive. In many ways, she is still a child trying to survive, never having the luxury of a carefree childhood.

Rosa came and stayed with us and helped us. Sometimes a week, sometimes a month, sometimes entire summers. She tried, she did what she could, and I respected that. A mother and a husband. We were both in absolute despair, but now we love each other. Or I can at least say that I understand and love Rosa. I think and believe and hope she loves me too.

In all honesty, this is what I wanted from my sister, my mom, and my best friend Erik too. I wanted them to fight for me. They needed to sacrifice something in their own day-to-day lives to help me, but they never did. But Rosa did. **True love.**

CHAPTER 114

THE MEANING
OF LIFE

I HAD BEEN CLOSE TO DEATH TWO TIMES IN ONE YEAR—THE car accident and the stroke. When you have been hit hard, you think a lot about why you are here, because you are in reality very close to the end.

It may be presumptuous to speak about, but isn't this what we all want to know? Isn't this what really haunts us all in our sleepless nights? Isn't this what we wonder when we look at our husband, our children, our workplace, our money, our cars, our house? We wonder, "Is this it?" Is this the meaning of life? Aren't we all rushing through our day, filling our days to not have to think about just that?

The meaning of life is what engulfs you, what makes you lose track of time, what puts a smile on your face, what you lose yourself in. It can be your girlfriend or wife. It can be work, if it's a passion. It can be your pets. When your dog comes up and "paws you" and wants to play, licks you in the face, and barks of joy.

When your wife talks proudly about you to someone else. When you have fun with your friends and can be your absolute self with them. When you lose yourself in your film editing and the hours float by. When you run and experience the runner's high. When you swim with your eyes closed and feel like you are floating in space. That is life. Whatever makes you be present, right here and right now, enjoying the moment, not dwelling on the past, not planning the future, when you are present with yourself and in sync with time. Because there really only is here and now.

What else are you looking for? What else do you think is out there? Eternal bliss? What does that mean to you? Is that your soul floating around in a weightless state in the skies? But will you really be happy? Isn't the body tied to so much of what is you and what you know? Without your body, you won't be able to see, feel, or touch. It will just be a dark consciousness floating around. I know you dream about meadows and a father figure in a white beard, but I beg you not to give up on this life to wait for the elusive afterlife. You may be missing out on one of life's most precious gifts: life itself.

To be connected. To be part of a community, a family, a yoga class, a runners' club, to interact, to feel, to talk, to have someone to call, or to just come over and hang. That is life.

I think most people misunderstand the word *meaning* in the phrase "the meaning of life." They should consider their purpose and make sure their purpose includes a lot of responsibility. Through responsibility, you will find appreciation, self-worth, and respect, all while doing good for someone else. True meaning (purpose) is always doing something for others.

The meaning of life is also to find yourself, like I have. I hope you find yourself without going through the fires I did. Once you find yourself and you respect yourself, you can stand naked in the street with absolutely nothing and still be content and happy with no fear of death.

Heather, my yoga teacher, asked me about my thoughts on the subject. She had a client making more than a billion dollars in sales, and he had asked her, "Is this it?" as in, "Is this all life has to offer?" I had been there too. Before the accident, I was at one point making much more than I could spend. That's when I started doing custom-built furniture, moved into a huge place, upgraded the car, etc.

I remember asking myself exactly the same thing, "Is this it?" The money did not fulfill me. In fact, I was lonelier than ever.

Now I know what was missing, I always knew. It was what I had been looking for since childhood—family, community, and deep connections with people. We are social animals, and we need each other to feel good. We need to feel we belong and that we are needed. Money has absolutely nothing to offer when it comes to this.

The one thing the accident gave me was just that. It gave me a family of friends and a community with deep connections. I have friends who will walk over fire for me now, and I will do the same for them.

If you are lonely right now, find your people. What are you interested in? Whatever it is, find out where you can meet people who share your interests. When you meet them, be courteous and give from yourself. Ask them about their lives and listen to them. If they ever ask you for a favor, just do it. Establish trust and show them you are a person of your word. That will give you a family, a community, and a happier life. Trust me on this.

CHAPTER 115

I ONLY RESPECT TWO PEOPLE

I HAVE BEEN THROUGH HELL, AND BY NOW, YOU KNOW IT TOO. We are deep into this story, you and I. Don't worry, I won't take you too far out on the deep end, but I want you to know enough to help you or your loved one. We have already established that it takes honesty, truth, and responsibility, but I must carry on a little bit further for you to understand fully.

Early on, walking on the beach with my halo screwed into my skull, I was searching for answers. I listened to thousands of hours of podcasts. The one that stuck with me was Dr. Jordan Peterson. Not the book he got famous for, *12 Rules for Life*. No, I listened to his early material, the university lectures he held for his students. They are so raw and honest. Later, I dove into his biblical studies, and I consumed absolutely everything he had done that was available online.

This may seem hard to understand, but what hooked me was how he had explored the evil of mankind, writing an essay about the Nazis at a very young age, and how he acknowledged, embraced, and promoted that life is hard and full of suffering. If there is one person who helped me get through the early years after the accident, it is Jordan Peterson.

Here was someone who praised hard work, had explicit insight into darkness, praised family, didn't search for happiness, but searched for meaning that you get with responsibility. That is what I needed to hear. I needed someone real. Dr. Peterson became my soothing voice of comfort while he was talking about how evil mankind can be and how life is suffering.

The second person came later. David Goggins. A powerhouse of mental will and determination. What appealed to me was the fact that he challenged himself, every day. He was living my life. I had to get up and face my demons and face what happened to my wife, every day, and so did he, voluntarily.

David is a former Navy SEAL, Army ranger, and Air Force TacP (all Special Forces). He has done numerous grueling ultra runs (runs over fifty, a hundred, two hundred miles) and continues day by day to push himself.

You see, I don't respect words alone. They are just words. Words mean nothing without the intention of doing and the actual doing itself.

CHAPTER 116

FIGHT YOUR INSTINCTS

Two people called me wise—my ex-wife, Pauline, and my dad.

I have listened to over 2,000 hours of podcasts these last five-plus years. My focus has been on doctors, neuroscientists, athletes, astronomers, philosophers, and psychologists. My own situation is uniquely mine, and what I do daily is put a lot of these theories in practice in real life.

And I challenge myself. I challenge myself to listen more, learn more, and I continuously challenge myself to live up to my new me. A giving me. I fall and stumble all the time, but I am here—I am still here.

My worst fear is that something happens to me and I can't take care of Kat. I imagine her lying in bed, lifeless, crying, and no one is there. It breaks my heart to think about it. I am writing this paragraph in May 2020, in the midst of the coronavirus pandemic. The coronavirus worries me.

During the years after the accident, I have posted on Facebook daily. It became my way of healing, my way of crying, my way of venting. I posted my concerns about dying before Kat, and she commented on Facebook, "Don't worry, babe, if you go before me, I will go soon after," and it gave me comfort. It did.

CHAPTER 117

A THOUSAND MILES AWAY AND KAT NEEDS HELP

Year four was coming to an end. I was lying in a hammock in Belize. White sand, red hammock, blue skies, and green water. I had a drink in my hand and life was good, until it wasn't.

Fiora, one of our day nurses, FaceTimed me from thousands of miles away in Los Angeles. "Kat is overheating. What do we do?" I see that she is driving and someone else is holding the phone. "Where is Kat?" I ask. The phone pans over to the back and I see Kat lifeless, her head hanging like a ragdoll.

I tell them, "Go home. Do not go to the ER. It will take too long, and they don't know what to do."

Go home! I keep them on the line while I send out a group text to my friends. "Need help! Kat is overheating. Need help at our house now!"

Who would answer such a call? Turns out, everyone would.

Heather, my physical therapist and yoga teacher, dropped everything at work and set course for my house. Rachel, one of the owners at CrossFit Divinity, came first. Chris, shortly thereafter. When Fiora pulled up, they carried Kat into bed and literally bathed her with ice cubes to get her temperature down.

I was witnessing it all on FaceTime, thousands of miles away in a tropical paradise. It was one of those times I thought Kat might die, but friends came for her. Friends came to save us. **True love.**

Being that far away when this happened was excruciating, and I felt helpless and overwhelmed.

CHAPTER 118

YEAR FIVE, IT ALL COMES TOGETHER

WE MADE IT FIVE YEARS. THAT WAS NEVER A GIVEN.

Do we need trauma to be enlightened and actually be able to change? It seems that way. Too many say the words but do not do the actions needed (until something major hits them or the ones they love).

I have met a few people with old souls. Pauline, my ex-wife, is one of them. They seem to have the ability to see right through you without having experienced trauma. It makes me wonder about rebirth. I am spiritual. I believe we are a closed ecosystem here on earth, so it would make sense that all that energy is not dead when we die but gets reborn in another form or shape. It is sort of self-fulfilling, but Pauline believes in rebirth too.

I am not afraid of death anymore, mostly because I see it as liberation, but if we do get to get reborn, I hope Kat gets to walk and run again.

As the years have gone by, I have become more and more philosophical about these things. I think a lot. I guess I am still looking for an explanation, which I know I will never get.

CHAPTER 119

THE APOLOGIES

It took five years.

I answered the phone and a woman said, "Are you Pavel?"

I said, "Yes."

She said her name and said she was speaking on behalf of Rosa. She was a counselor, a healer of sorts, who said Rosa didn't want it to come out in broken English, so she was to be Rosa's voice.

I was very suspicious and said, "Okay?"

And then the world stopped moving. The lady said, "Rosa doesn't blame you for the accident anymore. She understands it wasn't your fault."

Kat was listening in on speaker phone, and we looked at each other in disbelief. I heard Rosa cry in the background, and I asked her to come to the phone.

I said, "Thank you for allowing me to listen to you the last time you were here, about your childhood, about your struggles."

Shortly after this, Kat also cryingly apologized for lashing out at me in anger. She said she had forgiven me but deep down unconsciously blamed me. PTSD is ever-present with Kat, and it makes you say and do things out of sheer pain.

I'm glad I held out and got to live through these moments, if only just for me. Trust me, it's not easy being a driver and having an accident.

In some ways, I felt free now. I felt free to leave if I wanted. I felt free in my mind. In some way, my debt was repaid. Five years. It took five years. I'm glad I held out.

I took their blame willingly because of what happened to Kat. Now that they understand it was not my fault, I have stopped. I don't call them out. I just look at them and walk away when they relapse. I'm an easy target when they get upset, but no more.

I have not stayed with Kat out of guilt. I am with her because I love her. I understand people need someone or something to blame. I've let my actions prove to the world who I am, and the world slowly came around.

I don't credit my survival to anyone but me. But it was my love for Kat that kept me together. It gave me purpose.

CHAPTER 120

MY EX-WIFE

PAULINE MESSAGED ME AND SAID, "IF YOU DIE, I WILL MOVE into your house and take care of Kat," and I believed her. She is the most courageous person I know. She only says things she means. Others have said the same, but I don't believe them. They don't believe themselves. It's just something they say. The truth is, without people like Pauline, Kat would end up in a nursing home if I die. Not right away, but eventually.

CHAPTER 121

COVID-19

THE MORE THE WORLD HURTS, THE BETTER I SLEEP. IT'S AS IF I am not hurting alone anymore. I've lived five years with this hurt —the uncertainty, the nagging feeling things will never be the same again. I know all about it. Adapt or die. Things will never go back to normal. There will be a new normal, but the more you wish for the past, the more you will hurt.

CHAPTER 122

MARTHA AND HEAVEN

I AM SAD TO TELL YOU THAT MARTHA PASSED AWAY THIS YEAR. I cried when I got the notice. I had met Martha on two trips, and she recognized me when I came back to her. It felt so good to be able to help her, but it wasn't enough. I suspect she gave up. When our will to live fades, the body follows fast.

She asked us to help pay for the funeral, for herself. Life can be so cruel that you have to ask for money for your own funeral. Thanks, Martha. Thanks for allowing us to help you. You gave us a purpose. We will help others in your honor.

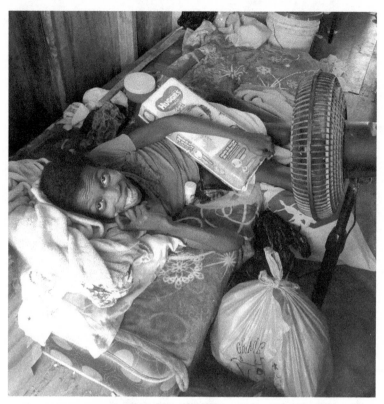

Martha, smiling. She spent most of her day on this mattress on the floor.

CHAPTER 123

EDDIE AND HEAVEN

SO I FINALLY STARTED LIVING THE LIFE I THINK I WAS ALWAYS meant to live. I just never knew how to get there, or how to set myself free to live it. Maybe I was a coward; maybe I just followed all the others in the rat race. Maybe my ego took over. I do think my ego took over and never let that other side out. The empathetic side.

Remember Eddie? I told you about him briefly in the beginning of this story. The night of our accident, Kat and I stopped by a private small party, Air Force friends of Kat who lived close by. We hung out in a small backyard bar in a lush house near the beach. I said hi to Eddie, was offered a drink, but I said, "No thanks, I'm driving," but I remember saying I wish we could stay. It seemed like they had so much fun.

The next time I met Eddie was in our Manhattan Beach rental home when Kat had just gotten home from the VA. I remember him commenting on my biceps and I laughed it off saying, "Look at you, big boy!" Eddie was well over 220 pounds and a big muscular guy then.

From left: 220lbs Eddie, Kat, and Eddie's two sons.

Another two years passed, and I was asked by Kat to pick up her friend at Cedars-Sinai Hospital downtown. He couldn't drive. He was going through chemotherapy. It was an hour and a half drive there, but I gladly accepted. It was skin and bones Eddie; it was Eddie with stomach cancer. A 140-pound version of Eddie with dark glasses because the sun hurt his eyes.

He said, "You probably don't remember me, but we've met."

I said, "Kat told me we had met. How are you feeling, brother?"

If I was religious, I would say it was meant to be to have our lives intertwined like that. Somehow, there was a lesson in all of this. But the pain I saw Eddie go through from that moment till his death bed, the pain he saw in Kat and me, I wonder, what's the lesson to be learned from all of that?

All that comes to mind is grace. To live and die gracefully and with honor. In the end, it is all we have. We only have ourselves and how we behave in the world. I loved Eddie for allowing me to be with him during his last year. I drove him to appointments, hung out at his place, and talked.

We didn't have the same interests, but I wasn't afraid of him. I was trying to be to him what I needed others to be to me. I was trying to be the friend he needed. He too had a best friend who abandoned him the minute he got sick. I was one of five people he requested to be at his cremation. Imagine the honor.

Neva, his girlfriend, married Eddie the day before he died. They had been together for a long time, and it was beautiful. I made Eddie smile.

I said, "What have you done, bro?" (Referring to getting married.)

He laughed, lying in his hospital bed chipping for air. That smile is what I am so proud of. Neva gave me some of Eddie's clothes and his bicycle. I wear his clothes a lot. They give me strength, and I ride his bike with pride. As I sit here in the wee hours of the morning, I am wearing his blue Columbia lumberjack shirt. It's big on me. Eddie was bigger than me. I guess I will have to grow into it.

People ask us, "How long were you married before the accident?" One year for me and Kat. Eddie and Neva got one day of marriage. I know why people are asking, but bliss and happiness is not in that one year or one day. The bliss is in everything we do together, and everything Eddie and Neva did together, and everything we do to still honor him. They got to fight together and prove themselves, just like Kat and I are fighting together and proving ourselves, to ourselves. That in itself is a gift as you get to know yourself. Who you really are.

140lbs Eddie and me, hanging out at our house.

CHAPTER 124

GOOD AND EVIL

GOOD AND BAD ARE ALL WITHIN US; WE JUST CHOOSE WHAT to cater to and what to develop. I have gotten to know the human spirit well by now. I have talked to other trauma victims, and I have read a lot of stories. Most have one thing in common. Family and friends abandon you. They want no part of it. It is a recurring theme throughout everything. On the flip side, the ones who stay or the ones who come to help become your new family and probably the family you always wanted and needed.

It is cultural, to an extent. In the Nordic countries, we place our elders in long-term nursing facilities and visit them in the beginning and then far and few visits between. In the Spanish-speaking countries, many families live like large families from cradle to death and help take care of each other.

I always dreamt of a big, loving family, and I have that now with Kat, her mom Rosa, four Yorkies, and all our Angels in Matt, Pauline, Chris, Eddie, Ted, Detra, Marcia, Evan, Star, Cherrie, Ancona, and four nurses on a never-ending 24/7 schedule. **My white picket fence life.**

CHAPTER 125

THE COMEBACK

Neuroplasticity. The brain's ability to change. It's plastic. It is ever changing, ever learning. Someone sent Kat a video clip of a doctor doing work with paralyzed people in Colorado. She worked with them in the hot springs and had a whole methodology based on the paralyzed person watching a moving person in front of them and trying to imitate that person's movement. The warm water makes it easier to move and helps the healing. The amazing part was that the video clip showed people actually being able to move again. People had regained mobility!

Kat reached out to the doctor via a friend of ours, and through sheer luck and timing, Kat was chosen among tens of thousands to partake in the doctor's program. Kat started the program remotely via phone while we waited for the COVID-19 pandemic to settle so we could travel to Colorado and partake in the whole program.

Kat was fighting again! This was the first time in five years Kat had been talking about real hope, mobility, and was actually doing the work to try to get there. It was not Kat's fault. After the accident, and after she got home, everyone said she was lucky to be alive, but there was nothing to do to regain movement.

She didn't give up. We researched stem cell therapy, and we applied for different trials, but none panned out in the end, either for financial reasons or due to Kat's injury not being the type of injury that particular trial was focused on.

We tried to implement water rehab the best we could, waiting for COVID to subdue so we could go to Colorado and train with the doctor.

CHAPTER 126

DR. MURPHY

I SAW DR. MURPHY JUST THE OTHER DAY. HE CAME TO OUR house. Five years had passed, but when we met, it was like yesterday. If it wasn't for people like him, I don't think I would have made it. The right people have the ability to power you just with their words and their belief in you. They see something in you and they bring it out of you.

Remember the money he gave me in the hospital five years ago? I gave it back to him. It is my time to give back now. I think that is what I am doing with Maynor and Martha in Belize, with Eddie in Los Angeles, and others I meet.

While I mourn Martha's and Eddie's deaths, I think and hope I've at least made their lives a little bit easier to live. I can be straight with people facing death, because I have been there, and I will not bullshit them.

CHAPTER 127

ANGST

TIME DOES NOT HEAL WOUNDS. WHAT YOU DO IS MANAGE THE pain. You are able to disguise your pain better and better, but the wounds are still there. Scratch a little bit, and the blood will start pouring out like it happened yesterday.

Real trauma, accidents, armed conflict, loss of a child—these don't go away. They burn themselves into your skull, and your neural pathways are there forever making you relive the moment over and over again.

The high suicide rate for veterans is proof of it. You may be able to change habits and quit smoking and start to exercise or eat less food. But real trauma is there for life. This is why I don't want to live forever. When it is time to go, I will do so willingly. No one can take this much sorrow every day.

CHAPTER 128

KAT WANTS TO DIE

KAT SCREAMS AND CRIES FROM THE BOTTOM OF HER INNER being. She is in her wheelchair surrounded by friends. It's late September 2020, and one of the first times we have had people over since COVID started.

Kat is tired. The isolation from the COVID outbreak and a caregiver that was performing subpar had Kat frustrated and feeling like a burden. She tells her friend, Star, her last wishes. Kat wants to go back to Belize one last time. She says when she dies, "Help find Pavel a wife so he is not alone." That is who Kat is, always thinking of others even when facing her own death.

Kat sits there among us. So sad. So tired, and we all understand. We are there, around here, taking turns comforting her. She yells out for her closest friends, Eddie Monge, Adam (her brother), and Chris. In this moment of utter despair, her friends are the ones she wants. I couldn't imagine a greater honor than to be called out for in this moment.

CHAPTER 129

TRUTH
AND LOVE

We are slowly coming to the end, you and I. Educating myself has been key for survival. Reading about others in similar situations, learning how they coped, made me stronger. I have a strong willpower—I know that. It was given to me, but I learned to hone it and to develop it.

If I could go back in time, I would, for Kat's sake. Obviously for Kat not to be paralyzed. But for me alone, I would stay in this reality. The man I am today is so much more than the man I was before the accident.

If people are given a choice, most choose blissful ignorance. They want no part of the pain it takes to develop yourself, and more importantly, to act upon your newfound knowledge.

I live my life, my truth, and it's based on love. Love for myself, love for my family, love for you, and most importantly, it's based on doing.

Words, intentions, and posts mean nothing. They change nothing. Doing is all that matters. I am not asking you to save the world, but maybe you can start by saying hi to your neighbor. Ask the homeless person down the street if he needs anything.

"The truth means responsibility. That's why everyone dreads it." The words are from a film I saw the other day, and it could not have been said better.

CHAPTER 130

BACK TO THE EMERGENCY ROOM

WE ARE ON OUR WAY TO LONG BEACH TO SEE OUR FRIENDS Eddie Monge and Alana. Kat says, "Lean me back," but her wheelchair is already leaned back as far as it goes. We pull over. She says, "Push on my stomach," and caregiver Lucia and I are pushing. It's been a while now, and we are getting worried. Normally it helps to lean the wheelchair back and give fluids.

We are on the side of the road. I decide to continue down to Long Beach. If Kat gets better, we will meet with Eddie, and if not, we have the VA's spinal cord unit, and the ER is close by.

Kat is not getting better. Lucia is in the back of the van, standing next to Kat. I take the driver's seat and we head toward the ER.

Kat can't see anything anymore. Her vision is gone. She is only able to hear. The pressure in her head is throbbing hard. We don't know this, but her blood pressure is near 200, and it seems to take forever to get to the ER. We are met by three people starting to ask questions about COVID in a leisurely way.

I scream at them, "This is a real emergency!" and just push myself past them.

We get a room in the ER ward, and I tell Lucia to go and get ice cubes. That normally helps. I talk to Kat, stroke her hair, and try to make her feel safe. Lucia comes back and says they won't give it to her.

I storm out of our room and start yelling at the nurses. "For God's sake, she will die."

They stay calm and try to calm me down, but I get more and more angry.

Turns out it was good that Kat did not get ice cubes. Her body temperature was 94 degrees and dropping while her blood pressure was almost 200 and refused to go down. Her body was cold and hot at the same time. Ice cubes would have shot her into hypothermia.

This was new. This was not good. A spinal cord unit specialist was called on the phone and they medically lowered Kat's blood pressure so she would not have a stroke. It took a while, but the blood pressure finally started going down.

I really thought I would lose Kat that time. Her eyes were empty, just like they were in the freezer at Costco. I knew the look of death all too well by now. Lucia, our day nurse, has done work in a hospice ward, so she stayed calm and collected. She even called Kat's mom.

Kat asked for Rosa at her worst, and we all thought that was the last call Kat would make.

When you feel death is close, all you want is a hand to hold or a familiar voice to listen to.

CHAPTER 131

HOKA HEY

YEAR FIVE IS COMING TO AN END. WE LIVE DAY BY DAY, GRATEful for each day we have together.

I took on the responsibility of myself and my paralyzed wife. I didn't choose it. In hindsight, for me personally, it was the greatest gift of all. Caring for someone else is the greatest honor there is, and while doing so, you earn self-respect and purpose.

I know how it is to wait for death. I did once, on the side of the road, and I was not smiling. If you can smile in that moment when death comes calling, you have lived a good life. Next time it's my turn to die, I will smile. I remind myself every day to live for that moment. To live to die with a smile.

Hoka Hey, "live so well that when your time comes, you die with a smile."

CHAPTER 132

BELIZE

Five years after the accident, Kat and I did what I wrote on Facebook that first night after I came home from the hospital.

> I will come back FUCKING STRONGER than ever!
> I will come back stronger for ME, for KAT and because there is no other way.
> We not only conquer, we surpass previous accomplishments and DEMOLISH THEM with new ONES!
> Watch us become STRONG again, watch us CONQUER!
> WE HAVE LIFE & we will be adventurous.

We boarded a plane to Houston and then to Belize International Airport. From there, we took a small island hopper plane to Kat's island "La Isla Bonita." We were adventurous again! We were back!

Belize 2021. Kat and me.

CHAPTER 133

THANK YOU

THANK YOU FOR READING THIS BOOK. I HAVE TRIED TO BE AS honest and truthful as I can be. That is what helped me get through the first five years. My hope is that this book will help others in our situation and raise awareness for spinal cord injuries in general and also give my answer to what love is and what the meaning of life is.

All proceeds from this book will go 100 percent to Kat's 24/7 care and well-being. If Kat passes away, proceeds will go to her foundation, Angel De Amor and be dispersed according to the foundation's wishes.

CHAPTER 134

A SELECTION OF FACEBOOK COMMENTS THAT SAVED ME THE FIRST FIVE YEARS

"The fire in your souls burns so bright when the two of you are together, and it shows in your eyes.

"You two have the greatest gift anyone could ever get in this lifetime. Many never get to feel the fires in their souls ignite, but you two burn so bright that you light up so many worlds beyond your recognition. I tell your stories to so many people. You two have taken on a hurricane and have rode the waves with such grace and beauty. We need real. We need heroes. We need people like the two of you to teach us to be those heroes."

—LACEY MARIE

"You came back a superman! A superhero! Kat's superhero! Because you are resilient and had love in your heart for me."

—KATHERINE PORTILLO

"You taught me the gentle spirit & iron discipline. You inspire, teach, and touch with your love and commitment to your beautiful wife."

—SHEVAUN WILLIAMS

"You are probably the strongest person I know."

—PAULINE NORDIN (FOUNDER OF FIGHTERDIET)

"I love your soul. Your love for Kat, your strength to overcome pain and darkness, your day-to-day battles, they're all so inspirational."

—ANONYMOUS

"I wish I had your strength."

—ALAN CUMMINGS (MARINE CORPS)

"Pavel! You are my hero! I can't believe you could do this with the HELL you've been through.

"MY TEN-YEAR-OLD SON DIED in a terrible CAR ACCIDENT only a few weeks before your accident. I have been following you and Katherine Portillo because your STRENGTH helps me keep going."

—RACHYMAMA

"Mr. Pavel Ythjall-Portillo, this message is to inform you of how much your sacrifices and daily efforts are recognized by your paralyzed wife.

"You now position items for her best use, like her phone, like it's second nature to you. You automatically pick the dry crusties from her eyes and still make her the best coffee. You happily help to orient the new caregivers and give positive feedback to the existing ones. You sacrifice your work hours for her care; whether to do a catheter,

transfer to/from wheelchair, feeding, driving, head scratching, and putting all the puppies on her lap.

"She admires how you stay healthy through exercising and nutritional intake (except jalapeño chips & whiskey). She loves how you are still interested in self-development and strengthening your marriage. Most of all she love your positive vibes and your charm. The word "Love" is just the beginning. Well, you are her favorite person in the whole, flat (j/k, wild, and round) earth! You are her 'media naranja.' Keep the adventurous coming buddy!"

–HER SINCEREST LOVE, KAT

"I watch both of you (Kat and Pavel) in awe every day via Facebook. You've met this unfair life challenge with such grace and fortitude... you are an inspiration to many, myself included."

–JEFF O'CONNELL (CHIEF EDITOR OF BODYBUILDING.COM)

"God damn, this is so powerful, your writing allows no prisoners or victims and is the message of pure WILL."

–HOPE ZARRO

"The strength, love, patience, and bravery you all emit is empowering. Even when you don't feel as though you are, you all are beautifully exemplary. Thank you for being real, being honest, and transparent. It is very humbling. All our prayers to you and yours."

–DANIELLE MITCHELL

"It must be a silent hell to feel Kat fade away. To know that you have done and still do and keep on doing all the best for her. It takes an emotional and concrete cost more than what can be expected. Shows *that your character has given you strength. U have chosen to help instead of fleeing or just dying. Respect and admiration all the way. I know, just words. The hug is for real."*

—DAD

"You two are the best example I have come across that identifies true love. Your relentless commitment to her and her outpour of will, power, and drive to live. Love you guys."

—ETNA MARES

"Your #1 fan and I always will be. Some days I look back and I KNOW u saved my life. U are my biggest inspiration and i will always look to you when i need inspiration or brought back to reality lol. Love u always, Pavel Ythjall."

—MARTY SANDER BUCKMAN

"The strength that you two show, even through the hardest of times, is amazing, admirable, and inspirational. I wish you both the best every day! And your raw honesty is greatly appreciated."

—MARISSA PFEIFFER

"Dear SON. U have made it for two years. U have, through that, become knowledgeable about yourself and the REALLY DARK PART of life...that could KILL A MAN. But u did turn it into STRENGTH...and still do, every day, day by day! Respect and admiration! U are THE BEST...and that's forever. LOVE YOU. BIG HUGS, DEAR SON, and keep on celebrating Christmas."

—DAD

"Pavel, you have taught me there is dignity & love in the midst of life's hell. Hoka Hey."

—SHEVAUN WILLIAMS

"I am so sorry, Pavel. I had never seen pictures of your vehicle after the accident. Seeing the aftermath... it just shed so much 'light' for me that I can't put into words. There is a reason your story & Kat's didn't end that night. I always believed it was because you two were & are meant to be living proof of what fighters are & what true inspiration is."

—IRMA GONZALEZ

"Most would have given up and walked away. Put their spouse in the care of the state and got on with their lives. Your love is stronger than those demons. We don't know what it is like for you to keep so busy that you don't shut down or they come out. I pray fervently for you. We love you both."

—ROBIN NICOLE

"You both show me daily, what true love really means. Your inner strength is powerful."

—JULES

"You have shown us, both of you, the power of the human spirit and what it truly means to love in spite of pain, near death, and injury. The body may break, but the spirit and your love for one another—never."

—KEO

"Hello, My name is Martha, I'm a daughter, sister, wife, mother of 3, and a personal trainer.

"This September, my 17-year-old son who was supposed to be enjoying his senior year in high school was diagnosed with an aggressive childhood cancer. He can no longer go to school or barely leave our home. He is struggling so bad mentally. We are living what seems like hell and struggle daily to keep fighting and keep things as normal as possible for our other 2 children. I just want you to know that you and your wife get me through my days. Your pain and strength is truly felt through all your posts and pictures and your love for each other is one of a kind. Thank you for sharing your story and your everyday struggles and your daily courage and strength. Thank you once again!

"Hugs,"

—MARTHA

"Only as a (spiritual) warrior can one withstand the path of knowledge. A warrior cannot complain or regret anything. His life is an endless challenge, and challenges cannot possibly be good or bad. Challenges are simply challenges. The basic difference between an ordinary man and a warrior is that a warrior takes everything as a challenge, while an ordinary man takes everything as a blessing or a curse."

—HEATHER

"I think you and Katherine Portillo are beautiful. You both make me a better person. I think about what you live with, and it has imprinted on my soul. I'm going home to my family in August, and I'm going to pray for all of us like I used to before my heart became so hard, you two give me faith in love. Thanks for living with such vigor. It's contagious and brings me back to that place, pushing me daily. Big hugs to you and Kat. **Thanks Pavel.**"

—ANONYMOUS

"I think it was brilliant on your part to allow yourself to be so vulnerable—about all of it. I've never felt it was a 'woe is me' look at how hard my life is now. Your shares have been more like, 'look at what we have been through?!' And we are making it!! Yep—you've been disappointed by people, processes, pain... but perseverance has been the lesson for all of us. We all learn from each other... even when we are pushed away by those we love. We get tough or we die. You both got tough. FB was an open diary. An accountability journal, perhaps. But I think it was brilliant to share because keeping it all in may have been your demise. It's always through the pain IF we can push through it, that allows our biggest opportunities for growth. HOKA HEY"

—LINDA LEWIS

"Your love for Kat gives me hope in humanity. Love like that is few and far between, and the people that hold such capacity for love, selflessness, and generosity are so rare.

"The love you two have for one another melts my heart, and it's nearly permafrost these days. You two are such a beautiful example of yin yang. Two halves of one whole. I have learned so much about love seeing the way the two of you love one another. When one contracts into themselves and begins to lose their grip, the other extends their reach and strengthens their grasp. Thank you for sharing such raw emotion and the divine aspects of the light and dark side of love with the world. You've shown the world that the dark side of love should be cherished just as passionately as the lighter side that humanity has chosen to romanticize to such a fault that the majority dismisses or demonizes the darker side and its transitions love has with your soul when it's experienced in the yin state.

"The fire in your souls burns so bright when the two of you are together, and it shows in your eyes. You two have the greatest gift anyone could ever get in this lifetime. Many never get to feel the fires in their souls ignite, but you two burn so bright that you light up so many worlds beyond your recognition. I tell your stories to so many people. You two have taken a hurricane and have rode the waves with such grace and beauty. We need real. We need heroes. We need people like the two of you to teach us to be those heroes.

"I hope your fires forever burn and light your way with the warm and glowing embrace of the coals that burn deep and unquenchable in the fires of your soul. The flow you two have found with one another has birthed such an infectious inspiration in not only the Fighterdiet community but the souls that we are all fortunate enough to share your story and pass your strength on with.

"I believe Kat's strength and your passion will forever proliferate and flow through the universe and touch many souls in this lifetime directly and indirectly as well as the lifetimes to come and the souls to come with it."

−LACEY MARIE

"It's people like you that should be running countries, negotiating with the powers to be. For you know real struggles, real sacrifice, you know what real love is and what it truly takes to survive at all costs."

−MARK TAYLOR

"You two are a true love story... love stories are not about the joy but the battles you fight each other and how you care for the other one."

−NORMA BRETTON

"I wanted to thank you on behalf of every woman for looking out and loving her like you do.

"I know it's not easy every day.

"Since what happened to the both of you, I no longer aspire for the type of love you see in cinema but the type of love you guys have.

"Truly keep being you."

—KEENDER BUENO

"You know what I thought... that Kat did get all the love and 'family' she always wanted more than anything... she's in a 'baby state' needed ALL from others... as sad as it is, she's in the center to receive love, support and friendship. Thank you for being the only man I know [who] would stick around."

—PAULINE

"Thank you all for the love ♥ Especially the love from my husband Pavel Ythjall ♥ When I feel strong and have the courage to live, it's because of your unconditional. ♥"

—KATHERINE PORTILLO

"This is true love ♥ most men would have run like a coward and found 'comfort' in another woman's bed... boohooing as to how sad it was to lose his wife to an accident.

"I've been following these two for over 10 years, separately at first, when they were both single to when they started dating to wedding to accident... that changed everything, to today! I've donated. I've supported them even though they don't even know who I am.

"He never left her side and still hasn't. Blessed is a woman whose man grabs her hand during hard times and says 'buckle up baby, it's about to get bumpy and I'm not going anywhere.'

"In my heart I truly believe that Kat Portillo-Ythjall WILL walk again through nanotechnology and stem cell therapy!"

−EVE TIMMERMAN

"I've often wondered who people truly are once everything has been taken away—Undeservingly yet you and Kat prevail with an overflow of the true riches which cannot be stolen or taken away! Kat's entire life has been the Epitome of a Warrior Spirit!"

−DETRA GILLETT

"I was called into a double trauma that night, husband and wife after a motor vehicle accident. The wife's imaging findings were concerning and she was noted to be paralyzed from the neck down. I went to her bedside immediately. Sadly, my neurologic exam confirmed that she had no movement from the neck down. I reviewed her imaging once more. I knew the chances were almost impossible for any meaningful recovery, but I was there to give her every chance. I offered them emergency surgery immediately to decompress, realign and stabilize Kat's spine. I told her husband that she was paralyzed and we could not expect that would change after surgery, but that we would mobilize the operating room team to operate on her emergently to do all we could to decompress, realign and stabilize her spine so as to maximize the chance for any recovery, however impossibly small that chance was. The goal of surgery was to enable her to sit upright in a wheelchair, to stabilize her neck to maintain the weight of her head when upright. We did not realistically expect her to regain her motor and sensory functions, though no effort was spared to operate on her emergently to give her every chance, no matter how remote, at recovery. Before he agreed to surgery, I reminded him again that his wife was paralyzed and would likely remain that way even after major surgery to avoid any misunderstandings in the high likelihood she would not improve postoperatively.

"His obligation to her, despite his own injuries and disabilities, was to remain strong for her, which I emphasized. There was no other role that was justifiable for him. While they were both victims, he was given no opportunity to take on self-pity. He immediately had to take on the role of supporter for her sake. I wanted to get to surgery immediately and did not want to waste a moment. At the same time, I wanted badly for him to know where things stood and what his wife needed of him in no uncertain terms, in the clearest and most concise terms as we rushed her to surgery. We spent hours in the operating room to treat her fracture dislocation. While the surgical goals were met, she did not regain her pre-accident functions. While we guessed this would be the case even before her surgery, the devastating reality had now manifested and we looked to her husband to live up to the role we had prescribed for him. He did not disappoint. Eventually he walked out of his hospital room and into hers on a different floor to spend time with her and to support her. While still a patient himself with a severe cervical spine injury, he had already begun his lifelong privilege of being Kat's caretaker.

"And then there were all the emotions the hospital staff had surrounding Kat. Her condition was all the more painful for all of us involved in her care because we quickly learned her life story and all the Herculean challenges she had surpassed even before this disaster— turmoil and abuse by her family, escape to the United States where *instead of taking on a victimhood mentality she took on the incredible role of contributor, leader and inspirator as she proudly served in the military. Her bravery—psychologically in her own country as well as in the US as an esteemed member of the armed forces—stunned us all. But we all knew that would pale in comparison to what was now being asked of her—not only to survive, but to find a way to enjoy this life in her new condition. She would need to draw upon her prior experiences and then some. She would need the reinvention of her husband to be her rock and supporter, caretaker physically and psychologically, in a way no one could imagine. We all thought it was impossible for them to make it, but we never said it.*

"A while later I saw them both at a party for trauma patients. I saw Kat in her wheelchair, disabled physically. Again, I wondered to myself how long she could survive this way, psychologically hurting from the physical state she was in.

"Years later, her husband found me. He recounted to me the extraordinarily difficult years they had shared—misery from dealing with the smallest details to the biggest ones. Chores building up. No qualified caretakers. Financial destitution. No family support. Despite being stripped down to nothing, these two were left only with their determination to survive. This determination was stronger than any material element or physical thing. This determination ultimately became the reason why they not only survived, but thrived. And I was lucky enough to take a back seat and watch the situation evolve into one of the most beautiful stories ever told."

—NEUROSURGEON FOR KAT AND PAVEL
(IN THE BOOK WE USED A PSEUDONYM)

RESOURCE SHEET

FILMS

The French movie *The Intouchables*.

The American remake of *The Intouchables, The Upside*.

REHAB

NextStepfitness.org

NextStep is an internationally recognized nonprofit organization that makes life-changing rehab accessible and affordable to those living with paralysis.

WHEELCHAIR HELP

The Wheelchair Foundation

THANK YOU

To my adventurous wife.

To my first beta reader, Anne-Marie Nordin Nilsson, and her daughter Pauline Nordin.

To my author colleague and beta reader, Barbara Golf.

To editor Stefanie Newell.

To the people of Ambergris Caye for always making me feel like I am one of their own.

SCRIBE.

CPSIA information can be obtained
at www.ICGtesting.com
Printed in the USA
BVHW081043231121
622336BV00008B/156/J

9 781544 523965